Goodbye
Little Town

Goodbye
Little Town

H. GORDON GREEN

McCLELLAND AND STEWART LIMITED
Toronto / Montreal

The Canadian Publishers
McClelland and Stewart Limited
25 Hollinger Road, Toronto 374

PRINTED AND BOUND IN CANADA

Chapter One

✤✤✤✤✤✤✤✤✤✤✤✤✤✤✤✤✤✤✤✤✤✤✤✤

A man isn't old, so the cheer-up people try to tell us, until his regrets take the place of his dreams.

I must be old now, for I no longer dream of going back and I regret the surrender of that dream so much that it is a kind of sad music in me. No, I have never held any grudge against the old home town for starving me out into the world, woodchuck fashion. For me, as well as the woodchuck, that was simply the way of the world. When a youngster had suddenly become big enough and brash enough, he had to shift for himself whether he wanted to or not. A young woodchuck got a somewhat better break than I did however. He could immediately dig in close by in the same hills of home, and indeed a young man born into one of the wealthier families in the village often had a chance to do the same. But I came from the wrong side of the tracks and before I could hope to establish myself comfortably among my own people I must go to the city where, so the bright legend assured us, the intrinsic justice of the free enterprise system could not be booted aside by such things as pedigree or piddling politics, and success was guaranteed to be in direct proportion to a man's capability.

So few of the farewell tears of that gusty February day in 1936 were mine. After all, it was only a matter of time until I would be back. I think I almost convinced my mother of that too. It was my grandmother who found the parting hardest and that came as an uncomfortable surprise to me because for all her tenderness, it was strictly against Grandma's tradition to be weepy. But she was eighty then. She had watched dozens of her grandchildren grow up and away and she had seen too many of these allegedly temporary goodbyes prove to be the last. Besides, I was a favourite of hers, "I think you ought to be a poet someday," she used to tell me. It was a strangely disturbing wish to come from a woman who had to sign her name with an X — something like that of a blind man wanting a son to become a painter.

She was right about that goodbye. It WAS our last, and it is ironical that it was the poet in me which was to blame for that. Because every young poet, whether he be guilty of verse or not, has at least one fatal flaw in his chromosomes — he believes implicitly in immortality. He can never really be convinced that Time is his master too. Tomorrow and tomorrow and tomorrow — the future stretches ahead of him like a pink infinity. And Time seems as limitless as his own possibilities.

But while I was so frantically trying to lay claim to those limitless possibilities, Time ran out for Grandmother, and she died before I could even afford the time for the first visit home. And long, long before I could afford the time to attempt that first poem for her.

There is nothing which provokes so many fierce excuses as an overwhelming sense of guilt, and when the message came I tried to tell myself that no one could have blamed me for staying away so long had they only known how it was with me then. Had they known that in order to earn the right to come home proudly and soon I had been working my way through University by joining the "graveyard shift" in a steel mill. The graveyard shift, in case you're wondering, is that ungodly eight hours in a factory schedule which begins at midnight. I began my classes at nine.

Poet I well might be someday, if part-time poets didn't become extinct by then. I was on my way now to becoming a doctor. A new doctor was one man who would always be welcomed in the old hometown.

Ah, had Grandma only lived another year! I thought. Because next year for sure there would be time and money for a quick trip home. It was positively disgraceful to exile oneself from one's family like this for two whole years, even for the noblest of dreams.

But "next year for sure" was postponed till the year after and then suddenly it was 1939 and every young man's dream in the world, noble or not, had to be stored away in the secret places of the heart till the lights came on again.

Afterward — five years afterward — it was too late to think of becoming a doctor, but the haunting compulsion to go back home was as strong as ever, and I wondered what other qualifications a man would have to acquire before he could hope to make a living in the old hometown?

After the Army gave me $100 and turned me loose, I went back there to see if there might not be some way now for me to make a decent living. Surely, I thought, a man in his prime and well broken to work should be able to find some sort of job commensurate with his ability. I was indeed so certain that my beloved town would take me to her heart again that I bought a house there. Bought the very house where my grandmother had brought her thirteen children into the world and where she had said that last goodbye to me ten years previously.

And again, I nearly starved.

Now had I been a more logical man I would have abandoned the idea then and there, but there must be something in this urge to return to the womb which is quite beyond logic.

"Even if you did find a job here," my wife told me as she started to pack, "it would never pay you half what you could get in the city."

Which I knew to be almost true, but had that half-pay job presented itself the year after the war ended, I think I would still have been under my grandmother's roof and there would have been no need then for me to write this book. But I would not abandon the idea, and all these years between, always, always, in the unchangeable part of my mind was the conviction that someday when I had a little more money, or someday when the children would have outgrown our obligations to them, I would go back to the old place and plant myself there even if I had to pay dearly for the privilege.

Why should so impractical a dream die so hard and with so many regrets? I don't know why. In my own defense I can only remind you that many a man who has made his fame or fortune being practical has been driven by this same obsession. The most famous economist this nation ever listened to will be remembered far longer for his nostalgic affection for the small-town people he had left behind than for anything he taught us about how to manage money, or even for his rare gift of humour. And long after the computors and the governments have insisted upon managing the last of our money problems for us and his humour has become stale and corny, our great-grand-children will still be reading about Leacock and his beloved Mariposa. Because Leacock is one of the few who brought that beautifully impractical dream down from the clouds. He did go back.

Henry Ford, on the other hand would never admit that going back was impractical at all, and as long as he lived he stubbornly maintained that more Americans, millions more of them, ought to go back. "When the problem of the city becomes bad enough," he said, "we will solve it by leaving the city."

Maybe it is time right now for us to make the move. As I write this, the city of Boston is in a turmoil because it doesn't have any place to put its garbage. For many years an off-shore island of fifty-some acres has been used as the city dump — a spot which Bostonians aptly refer to as "Spectacle Island." And even in these days, when we gift-wrap our garbage, that dump must indeed be a spectacle because the city's sanitary engineers have revealed that the accumulation is now forty feet high — so high that it is just too costly to pile it any higher. Nor is it safe.

That sad little bit of current history is merely one more proof that our half of the world has now come to the place where we can no longer ignore the chaos which always seems to threaten when cities get too big. Nor is it only the older cities like Boston which are so rapidly becoming intolerable. The current urban sickness of our day even extends to the majority of our new suburban developments. I have just learned that the sociologists have coined a new word to describe these suburbs — "slurb" — meaning, so I am told, sloppy, sleazy, slovenly, slip-shod semi-cities.

There seems to be no witty new terms yet to describe the more wretched aspects of modern, well-planned super cities, but this undoubtedly will follow. In 1880 the city of Los Angeles had only ten thousand inhabitants and, so everyone supposed a gold-lined future. Nothing could stop "L.A.", the inhabitants proudly declared. Not even a San Francisco earthquake. And in a sense they were right. Today Los Angeles has a population of seven million and, according to its own Chamber of Commerce, it is the fastest-growing city in the world now and will be the largest in the world by 1975. And in that incredible city is just about anything that is supposed to make the American way of life glorious and fat and free. Most important of all, there is space, elbow-room, sixty miles of it in fact, with the ocean on one shimmering perimeter and the mountains on the other. Some of the boulevards are forty-five miles long with house numbers running up as high as 35,000. And, as if determined to avoid the jam-packing of less fortunate cities, Los Angeles has set aside two-thirds of its downtown area for the automobile — parking lots, service stations, and drive-ins beyond count. But the famous freeways which were supposed to provide the long-sought answer to the traffic problems haven't solved a thing. They merely try a little harder with every passing year and battle their way a little farther out toward the mountains as if to get a breath of fresh air. For the smog thrown up by all this progress is so bad now that it is difficult to see how human eyes and lungs can stand any more of it.

The last time I was in Los Angeles one of the hit songs which was then being urged on us by the entertainment industry was joyfully proclaiming that "on a clear day you can see forever." It was a curious song, I thought, to come from this city where you could hardly see your hand in front of your face.

Surely we must now realize that we cannot go on making our cities bigger and bigger, blithely leaving the resulting mess for God and the politicians to solve. Even more perilous are the efforts now being made by some of our governments to urge the small, poverty-haunted farmer to move off his land and make way for someone who can actually make money out of that land because he has money to begin with. Certainly we must sympathize with the little man whose farm no longer allows him to provide for his family decently. But what favour do we grant him or the nation when the only other place ready to receive him is a city slum?

I am not as naive as to foresee a mass return to rural life. There are far too many of us now, and we have become too lazy. But I think that the small town may ultimately help us find the answer to the dilemma just as Henry Ford predicted a half century ago.

So the tears in the title of this book are not for the passing of the little green-circled country town as a design for living, because I am sure that we cannot afford now to let it die. The goodbye of my title is merely for that particular town in which, as one of the Almighty's favourites, I was permitted to grow. I have always lived in a small town or on the edge of one. Even in those hectic days when I had to travel forty miles a day to a city desk, I never for one moment contemplated the city itself as a place to live and raise a family. And I find it difficult to believe that if our changing way of life suddenly put small-town living within the reach of all, any enlightened and conscientious parent would still choose the city as the place to rear their children.

It doesn't surprise me at all that we are now witnessing a mass migration of families from the city and that big business is not only following gladly with its shopping centres but is indeed sometimes leading the way. But I am certain that of the millions which will leave the city within the next decade or two, many a family is not going to stop when the moving van comes to the nearest convenient suburb. It will not be content until it has found that home of its dreams in some sleepy little village which the maps have all but forgotten.

I would eagerly look forward to such a migration if it were not for one thing, and that is my fear that these newcomers will not be satisfied to leave the small town as they find it, but will immediately try to make it conform to the conscience of the city. They will want to tie up the dogs, outlaw the sheep, import a cop and a playground supervisor, complicate the building restrictions and make it illegal for a rooster to crow before eight in the morning. Above all, I am afraid that they will object to those very qualities which make the small town's way of life unique and wonderfully precious. I am referring to its neighbourliness and its refreshing lack of conformity. I am afraid that when these forward-looking city people join us they will mistake our neighbourliness for gossip and think our lack of conformity regrettably anti-social; and that would be a great tragedy. For there is no other community left to us, I think, where man still finds it possible to be both a good neighbour and an individual.

I am deeply concerned at what the loss of neighbourliness is doing to the essential character of America these days. This morning as I sat down to my coffee and porridge the radio told us that at long last one of the world's most famous murder suspects has been apprehended. This was the man who in 1964, on the sidewalks of New York, stabbed a girl to death while thirty-eight witnesses let her frantic pleas for help go unheeded because not a one of those thirty-eight wanted to become involved. And lest we Canadians protest that it can't happen here, let us remember that just three weeks previous to the capture of this man who murdered before an audience, a citizen named David Lumsden ran out into a Toronto street, naked and covered with burns, shrieking for help to get his wife and four children out of his burning home. Six cars ignored him and his family perished.

I wish I could comfort myself in the belief that such occurrences are always rare and far away, but I know they are not. Less spectacular examples of this same callous disregard of our fellow-men are on every side of us now. We have, indeed, now come to the place where we think it proper and right to ignore the other fellow. The police don't want us to pick up a hitch-hiker. Mothers don't appreciate the stranger who offers their youngsters a lift to the hockey rink. You aren't really contributing to charity at all anymore when you give a handout to a tramp; you are accused of aiding and abetting laziness.

What does such an attitude really prove about our generation?

A few evenings ago, on one of the bridges which connect the city of Montreal to a suburb, a teen-age boy stood beside a car which had pulled over to the curb and he was seen waving desperately for help. But one after another the cars whizzed by him with no regard at all for his distress. Nor do I doubt for a moment that each of those drivers thought he had a perfectly valid excuse for his disregard. "Not safe to pick up strangers these days . . . . Always suspicious of a boy that age begging for a lift. Never know who might have put him up to it. . . . Well maybe next time they'll have sense enough to make sure their gas tank is full before they start out. . . ."

The sad fact of the matter was that this young lad was neither a hitch-hiker nor had he been put up to anything. Nor was the car out of gas. What the passerby did not consider was the other person in the car. The boy's mother, who had been driving, had suddenly collapsed at the wheel. The son, thoroughly frightened and unable to drive, was doing the only sensible thing possible — he was doing his best to get help.

It was nearly thirty minutes before a police car came along. Had that squad car been headed in the other direction that night, so the doctors said afterwards, the stricken woman might very well have died right where she was.

I happen to have a personal interest in this event because, while I was not one of those Levites who passed by on the other side of the road, I know that several of my friends were. I know that because they were all on their way to a very important political meeting which was to be addressed by a nationally known figure, long noted for his courage and foresight in advocating social reform. Indeed, to those good friends of mine, the whole future of this nation depends upon this man's kind of vision.

Now, when one stands off a little way from an incident like this and begins to think it over quietly, doesn't it hold a sad sort of moral for us? Isn't it one of the more ludicrous aspects of human behaviour — and one of the most tragic — that we can be so fervently concerned with ways and means to mould the nation into a Utopia when we haven't even a proper concern for our next door neighbour?

Such incidents as those I have just related simply couldn't have happened in my home town because, though its other sins were often quite interesting, any lack of neighbourliness was something peculiar to snobs only. For above all else, ours was a village of chimney-watchers.

It should be explained perhaps to this thermostatically-comforted generation that chimney-watching was the simple act of looking out of one's window on a shivery morning to make sure that each of the chimneys within sight of you had a proper head of smoke on it. In any country village of those days there were a good many old people. Retired farmers mostly, or the widows of farmers who should have retired; and a chimney which didn't come alive in the morning was a distress signal which had to be explored at once.

This then is a collection of stories and comments about a chimney-watching town and the kind of characters I knew there as a boy. It may be wishful thinking for me to hope that my readers will find these characters as intriguing as I do, but at least they will find them different. For there isn't a character or yarn or story in this which could have been found anywhere but in a small town possessing that kind of individuality which I hope that progress will never be permitted to destroy.

There is one more thing I would like to mention. I have just found yet another reason for being glad that I put this book together. A few days ago I received my copy of my home-town newspaper. It is an eight-page chronicle, dealing with all those dear hearts and gentle people Bing Crosby likes to break into song about — even though some of them are anything but dear and gentle. Anyway, the paper is an unpretentious country rag, cosy with concern about bulls, boars and big potatoes, pee-wee hockey, auctions, church socials, and which of its citizens blew himself to a holiday in Toronto last week. Its format hasn't changed much since the days when, as a lad of eight or nine, I used to drop in on the way home from school and watch the editor and his man setting type letter by letter. No articles more than two columns wide and most of its front page just bits and pieces. To me it seemed that the weekly paper was as delightfully changeless as the village itself. It never got any bigger, the old familiar names were still there, and in every page there was the same lovely willingness to relax and let the rest of the world go by.

Imagine my shock, then, when I opened it up this week and saw a headline which screamed across the whole top of page one. It was the only headline I have ever seen in that paper. "FIRST INDUSTRY!" it said.

And I learned that, for the first time since it was cut out of the bush a little over a hundred years ago, the town is to have a factory; that the sod will be broken this spring for a thread plant. The building, so I was joyfully told, will be four hundred and seventy feet long, will operate twenty-four hours a day, seven days a week and employ eighty to one hundred people. I saw by the accompanying sketch that this tremendous institution will be erected on one of the fields where my dad and I once cut hay and pastured the cows.

Elsewhere in the paper, the editor rejoiced in the statistics his research brought to light. A hundred new wage earners in town will mean a hundred and twenty-three more school children; one hundred and thirteen more households; $356,000 more retail sales per year; four hundred and seventy more people, four more stores; one hundred and thirty-six more cars; forty more workers, employed somewhere other than in the manufacturing itself.

So it's hip-hip-hooray and a headline because this village, which in all the time I have known it has never boasted more than twelve hundred souls, is at long last going to get much bigger, and never again will anyone dare call it sleepy. But as I lean back in my rocker, I wonder what makes us so sure that bigger is better, or that faster means going farther, or that more getting and spending means more laughter in the streets or more love down the laneways.

Yes, Mr. Editor, I know it's progress and I patriotically salute the new day. But as one who has always loved the gentle quiet of your grassy streets and the fierce but wonderful independence of the characters who walked those streets in the humble days, I also lift my hat as to the toll of a funeral bell.

And after a funeral it is disgracefully easy to forget. . . . So now, whilst the memory of it is still warm, let me tell you how it was with my village in days before it had any pretensions of grandeur.

Chapter Two

❖❖❖❖❖❖❖❖❖❖❖❖❖❖❖❖❖❖❖❖❖❖❖❖❖❖❖

The town of Arthur is situated 72 miles north-west of Toronto. It is pleasantly located some 1,200 feet above the sea and is one of the best business centres in Wellington. This county, being named after Arthur Wellesley, Duke of Wellington, it was therefore thought fit and proper that our town should be called Arthur after the Duke's Christian name. . . .

. . . The early history of Arthur is shrouded in considerable mystery, as no reliable data is at hand or has been preserved for reference, so we are entirely dependent on the memory of the old settlers. Among the first settlers was the family of George Smith, who moved to Arthur about the year 1849. The place was then called Queen's Bush or Six Nations. As there were no "iron horses" in those days, it took just eight days to make the memorable trip from Toronto. The village had been surveyed in 1848, but the roads were very narrow through the bush, the surveyors following the old Indian trail, which is the cause why, to this day, there are so many bends in the main highway leading into Arthur.

. . . There were no stores in those days and the early settlers were forced to go to *Fergus or *Guelph for their supplies, and as they had no horses, all the travelling had to be done on foot. A settler who owned a yoke of oxen or steers was considered well off. There were no schools then either, but Mr. Smith, the early pioneer mentioned above,

---

*Fergus has always been a much more proper town than ours, perhaps because it is 12 miles nearer civilization. Guelph, 24 miles away, is our nearest city.

18

engaged an old gentleman to come and teach for six months. The books used were of the most primitive order, looking more like book covers. These had spelling on one side and reading on the other.

Since there were no clergy at hand in those days, it was a difficult matter for a couple to get married, for in order to get the ceremony performed, they would have to walk to Fergus. The clergy did, however, visit Arthur twice a year to administer the ordinances and preach. . . .

The first places of business in the struggling village were the hotels. In the matter of hotel accommodation, Arthur has always been well to the front. We are often reminded of the large number of small hotels and wayside inns which have passed out of existence in this end of the country. We can think of at least twenty of these which have had to close their doors within the past decade or so. In Arthur, however, hotel accommodation still remains a powerful drawing card for the commercial life of the place and today we have four hotels, all of which do a thriving business. . . .

(From H. E. Bywater's short history of our town, published in his weekly, *Enterprise News*, 1904.)

I have resurrected Mr. Bywater to show my reader at the very beginning of this book that in spite of all the rare and wonderful things I am about to tell him of my old home town, its history is quite without glamour, and that with one notable exception its origins are as humble and average as that of any other rural village in eastern America. I think that Mr. Bywater was beautifully subtle in his revelation of that one exception about our town — the fact that in the beginning was the hotel.

Now if you were to blow the dust from the early records of many of the less fortunate villages nearby, I am sure you would find a somewhat different genesis. First would come the mill, so that the wheat which was grown between the stumps would be ground into flour. And in our neck of the woods, where the first settlers were predominantly Scottish, that mill would also contribute to the chemistry peculiar to that dour race by providing oatmeal. Next, solemnly reminding its sons that man does not live by bread alone, nor by porridge either, would come the kirk. And for a long time the mill and the kirk were all that the settler had to help him in the struggle to carve himself a place in the sun. When the crops were good, he had bread and oatmeal. When the crops failed, he lived on the *Shorter Catechism*.

Then some missionary who wasn't a Presbyterian would come burning into the wilderness like a pillar of fire to strike off the damnable chains of apostasy. Which, to others whose zeal was still not satisfied, merely meant that there was now a second brand of error rampant in the settlement. Hence some other prophet would soon be led here by the Almighty to proclaim the *real* truth. By the time there were three or four churches the first store might appear, and then, if the churches were too busy battling amongst themselves to unite against the common enemy, the first hotel might roar into business.

In some communities however the new soil was so thoroughly seeded with sobriety that the hotel was never allowed to take root. For instance, in Fergus, which lies twelve miles south (biggest little town in Ontario, the signs used to declare), no tavern is to this day permitted to pollute the clean and prosperous atmosphere. For over a century now the nice people of Fergus have been stealing up the highway to Arthur to enjoy their brief respites from sanctity.

It is strangely fitting then that the very first place of business which welcomes the visitor coming up from Fergus or Guelph is the hotel. It is even more appropriate that the hotel should stand at one end of Main Street and that three of the churches should glare back in righteous indignation from the other. The inescapable cruelty of growing up in our town back in the '20's was that a lad was forever caught halfway between these two powerful and irreconcilable influences. And once, when I was trying desperately to resolve the battle of my own conscience, I asked my Uncle Yankee why he spent so much of his time and his money in the hotel. I was particularly troubled by my uncle's attitude because he admitted quite frankly that he not only believed in hell but was sure that he was going to end up there someday.

After all, Uncle Yankee rarely missed a camp-meeting.

Well then, I wanted to know, if he knew he was going to hell why didn't he do something now to change his course?

I remember that my uncle had just begun to dig a well for old lady Cashion the afternoon I asked him that and he had just dug himself into the earth far enough to bring his eyes level with my own. He had very blue eyes and very broad shoulders the same as all the rest of the Green boys. (There were ten of them till the war came.) And he never talked down to you or got sore at you for not remembering to address him as "Uncle."

"Yes lad," Yankee said leaning his chin on the end of the shovel handle for a minute, "I realize that there's a better place to go and I've thought sometimes about tryin' to make it. But from all the information I've been able to put together about how to get there, it looks like a pretty tough proposition. It's just as if — well now lad you've heard about the Grand Canyon in your geogriffy book haven't you? . . . Well now can you imagine a tremendous long cross-cut saw, long enough to reach from one side of that Grand Canyon to the other? And can you imagine that cross-cut saw stretched over the Canyon with its teeth pointin' up'ards? Well now lad that's the way I figure the straight and narrow way to heaven is. I reckon that there might be the odd person here and there that is just good enough to make a trip like that safe and no slippin.' But for me, I might just as well relax and spare myself the effort."

I must have been rather evangelical in those days because I distinctly recall the discomfort my uncle's reply aroused in me. "But Yankee," I persisted, "don't you know it gives you a bad name associating with the hotel-going kind of people?"

"Well lad," my uncle replied after thinking it over very soberly, "the way I figure there's really only two kinds of people a man can associate with in this here part of the country. There's the pious people and there's the honest kind. And I guess I prefer the honest kind even if they do give me a bad name."

Quite apart from the undeniably wicked brew which was stored in the barrels behind the bar, an Ontario country hotel of that time had a colour and a personality that our literature has no good reason to neglect. I am not sure what it was which fascinated me most about the old hotel when I was a boy. Perhaps it was the essential spirit of the place — that spirit of utter relaxation known only to those who cheerfully admit they are utterly damned. Or perhaps it lay in the fact that to the fuzz-cheeked lad of any age, nothing is so indescribably attractive as something which is strictly for men only.

Ah! the devil-may-care bull-throated masculinity of the place! Where you could swear any old time you felt like it! Where the younger customers could make salty comments and conjectures about all of the more interesting women in town, even the supposedly untouchable dames up on Crown Hill; and where the older men could volunteer unpublishable truths about the great people who, damn them to hell, happened to be running the country. Where, for a nickel, you could enjoy the rich, spotlighted green of the pool table and make the rainbow-coloured balls chase each other around as merrily as girls at a picnic. And I remember the big, age-stained prints of famous trotting horses long dead, the lacrosse sticks and deer horns, and the still savage wildcat which decorated the wall behind the bar; the horse-drawn bus which proudly wheeled up out front four times a day to discharge mysteriously important people just in off the train; the deer hounds stretched limp in the sun outside the big cool doorway. And then there was the livery stable out back with its rows of polished carriages at the ready, and the incredibly fleet trotters in the stable beyond the gently steaming manure pile. And beyond the trotters, secure in stalls of three-inch plank, were the arched and gleaming stallions, always at the ready too, always whickering impatiently through the stable port-holes when there wasn't enough love in the world to suit them.

The allure which a village hotel had to a growing lad was indeed so varied and so intense that a complete escape from it was practically impossible. For even if one fought off the sin of surrender, the temptation itself was enough to affect a man for the rest of his life.

My parents were very godly people — so God-fearing in fact that 'heck' was a swear word and a deck of cards a passport to perdition. So there was never any doubt in my mind then that the hotel, for all its attraction — or perhaps because of it — was inherently and unspeakably wicked, and that the men who went there were really whooping down the broad and slippery highway to hell.

One thing troubled me however. Why was it that if you really needed help of some kind — a lift home from school; your lacrosse stick strung; a home for your dog so he wouldn't have to be shot; or maybe even the lend of a quarter when you had busted a window at school and were going to get whaled if you didn't get it fixed — why was it that these hell-whoopers were much more apt to help you than the good and respectable people?

And even to this day, if you were a writer in search of the essential soul of a small town and the kind of characters who can warm the pages of a book, you would probably waste your time courting the confidence of the proper people of the community. Proper people have two great disadvantages so far as a novelist is concerned. They lack the courage to tumble into adventure and they lack the honesty to become lovable. So you would waste little research on citizens who own the town and that superior few who have the better stands on Main Street and the big stone houses up on Crown Hill. You would open your heart and your notebook to the little people; these ordinary imperfect impractical people who have long ago discovered that they aren't smart enough to pretend and have therefore no alternative but to be themselves even if it means the death of them through damfoolishness.

And nowhere will you find these ordinary, imperfect and impractical people so totally devoid of pretense and so completely surrendered to the fate of being individuals as in a small-town hotel. In my boyhood days the very fact that a villager would even dare the judgment of the great and the good to frequent the tavern was in itself a confession that he had a mind of his own and that impropriety was his chosen way of life.

As I remember all this, the span between now and then has widened to forty years and I have finally arrived at that comfortable age when my conscience no longer bothers to argue with me. I have come indeed to that stage in life where a man ceases to worry about how to avoid temptation and begins to wonder how much of it he may be missing. But though the home-town hotel is no longer labelled an outpost of the Outer Darkness, and has therefore lost its power to make me tremble deliciously with the siren lure of utter sin, I find that it still has a profound fascination for me. And the reason for this other fascination, I think, lies in the fact that so many of the villagers I remember best and most fondly were among its faithful patrons.

But I didn't intend this chapter to be an essay on country inns when I began it. What I really wanted to do was to tell you more about my Uncle Yankee, and in particular about a peculiar adventure which his damfoolery once got him into. The reason I was carried away by my memories of the old home-town hotel was simply because it was there — while he was enjoying a mug or two with some of the honest people — that this damfool adventure got started. Or perhaps it would be more accurate to say that it began in the livery stable behind the hotel where, in keeping with the defiant masculinity of the place, the innkeeper's line of massive draft stallions were quartered.

It happened one year that among these great studs was a Clydesdale by the name of Sir Craigie something or other, a magnificent animal who, when his knighthood was in full flower, weighed close to a ton.

The aristocracy of Sir Craigie's pedigree gave him a fame that few of our citizens could equal, and hundreds of the finest colts in the country were the fruit of his loins.

Came a day however when this stallion was no longer interested in improving the race, or very little else in life for that matter, so his owner suddenly found himself in need of a man with a talent for handling sad emergencies. "Yankee," he said, "if I were to give you a couple bucks, would you take this stallion out into the country somewhere and shoot him and bury him?"

"For a couple of bucks and a couple of drinks I might consider it," my uncle replied.

But after the couple of drinks had been thoughtfully stowed away in the company of a lot of other horse-minded men who remembered the days of Sir Craigie's glory, my uncle somehow came to the conclusion that this was really too famous a beast to be merely tossed into some desolate swamp and forgotten. So he swore one of the most honest of his drinking companions to absolute secrecy, and when the pair of them at last quietly slipped away from the hotel and out of town, they led Sir

Craigie in the direction of the Protestant cemetery which awaited the resurrection some two miles west.

"We'll bury him with full honours," my uncle had decided. "And on hallowed ground. It's what I'd expect for myself if I was ever to live such a distinguished life."

First, as the shades of evening gathered, they dug the hole while the old Clyde contentedly munched some grass from some of the graves a few rods away, which were badly in need of clipping. Then when the hole was thought to be deep enough, they led Sir Craigie over beside it, "Goodbye old lad," they said. "We're awfully sorry about this but you've got to admit that life was pretty good to you, don't you now? Anyhow, we'll be seeing you soon."

They gave him a last pat on the shoulder, and with a single well-placed shot, tumbled Sir Craigie feet up into his grave.

It was then that my uncle discovered to his discomfort that the grave was somewhat smaller than he had thought and that the stallion was considerably larger. Try as they did, the four shining shoes of the deceased stallion kept protruding at least eighteen inches above the level of the turf.

"Maybe the sun will shrink him somewhat tomorrow," my uncle's friend hoped. "Or maybe the grass is so long anyways that no one will notice."

My uncle was more realistic. "Maybe we can pile up enough dirt to sort of mound them feet over," he suggested.

But the feet didn't want to be covered over. The dirt kept rolling away from them as if it were kicked away.

It was getting dark; the two men were tired; and they kept thinking that they should really report back to the innkeeper now. He might be wondering what had happened to them. So they did the best they could with an impossible assignment, making a mound over the deceased that seemed higher than some of the tombstones in the occupied section up the slope. Finally they found a second-hand funeral wreath to give the grave a proper token of sympathy and then went back to town.

Bright and early next morning, the whole village was in an uproar. A certain influential lady on Crown Hill had absolute proof, so she declared, that my uncle Yankee had buried a horse in the Protestant cemetery, and she demanded that the authorities order said horse's removal immediately.

My uncle pretended to be quite perplexed when he heard of the complaint. "Well now," he said very seriously. "I'll admit that Sir Craigie was owned by a Catholic. But you're forgetting that this same stallion was bred by Bobbie McTavish, the same as happens to be not only a Protestant but an Orangeman and a Presbyterian as well! So how could you expect us to bury him in the Catholic cemetery?"

The great lady who had the absolute proof however, was not at all interested in the argument, be it humour or theology, and she soon had a dozen others to share her anger. Even the hotel-keeper, Irish though he was, refused to see anything funny about the matter. After all, some of his best customers were Protestants.

"You'll have to get that stallion out of there and fast, Yankee!" he said. "As a matter of fact, I think that the constable is looking for you right now!"

Gradually the desperate truth of the situation was inescapable. Sir Craigie had to be exhumed and his remains transported to some other part of the earth's bosom. But how in the world were they to lift a full ton of *rigor mortis* out of the grave? And even if they did find a way to lift it, where did they go from there? And how?

As soon as the bar opened in the hotel that day, a solemn and troubled conference was held between my uncle and every horse lover who would listen to his tale of woe.

"Now I know that I'm not up on my religion like I ought to be," Yankee said, "but are humans the only ones that's fit to be buried in a cemetery?"

"Sure now and this is no time to start any search of the scriptures, Yankee," the hotel-keeper said. "You finish that drink and get out there with your shovel before the law gets really mad at you!"

"Just suppose," said Yankee, "that the law was to put me in jail for this? And just suppose that after they did that, the law was still so upset about that horse that they decided to move it themselves? How would they do it? That's all I want to know. How do I move a ton of dead horse anyhow?"

There were some engineers in the tavern that day who thought that a block and tackle was the only answer, though everyone agreed that engineering a dead horse out of a grave with a block and tackle would make quite an unseemly spectacle. Therefore, if there were any other way of solving the problem it would probably be better to try and find it.

Someone else suggested that the only feasible solution would be to dig another grave beside the one already holding Sir Craigie, make this one real deep — maybe ten feet or more, and then tumble the stallion into it. Then, when he was buried, he would be so far underground that no one would ever be able to find him.

Yankee shook his head. This wasn't his lucky day, he said, and someone would be sure to discover the trick and tell on him. "Blast it all!" he said. "And all I wanted to do was to give the old boy a little glory and a decent goodbye!"

"Blast it!" someone repeated, a strange look coming over him. "Why not, Yankee? Why not blast him? It's the only way!"

Now it happened that among the many good Irishmen who lived in the old home town was a man by the name of Mike Gainer. Mike was a farmer now, but he had spent a good deal of his colourful life out in Montana somewhere. According to his own classifications, Mike had been a mule-skinner out there in one of the mines. Meaning that he drove the mules which pulled the ore cars. He was back home in the east now because the job had ruined his lungs.

"I'm going up to see Mike Gainer," Yankee said. "Anybody coming with me?"

So it was that curious group of characters went up to the Gainer farm that day and asked Mike for his advice. "You were skinning mules out in them there Montana mines, were you Mike?" Yankee asked. "You must know quite a bit about blasting too?"

"Sure and I could blast off the pyramids if you had the money to buy me the powder," came the reply. "Who do you want to blow up?"

"I've got five bucks here," Yankee said, "Do you figure that would buy enough dynamite to lift a ton of dead horse say five feet out of the ground?"

"It would do more than that," Mike said. "It would blow him into so many smithereens that he'd never have to be buried again. And we'd also have a little left over for a spot of celebration, I don't doubt. Only we better wait till tonight to do it, I'd say."

So the deed was done at night. Mike set his charges carefully, calculating the amount of dynamite that each boring should require and then putting in double to make sure.

Then when he lighted the fuse and they all joined in a strategic retreat, Mike suggested that each remove his hat and clasp it to his breast in an attitude of prayer. "Not just to bid the Lord's blessing on Sir Craigie," he explained, "but because there might be enough dynamite under him to lift the whole caboodle of us with him!"

The resulting roar, so it was said afterward, could be heard in Kenilworth, eight miles away. It also tilted a tombstone or two and broke a pane of glass in a nearby barn.

The way the story is told around home today is that Sir Craigie completely disintegrated. But that may merely indicate that the facts of the episode are fast growing into legend. The critics certainly don't believe that Sir Craigie's disappearance was a mere evaporation. They will tell you that the departed stallion was merely reburied on the installment plan.

In any case there were no enemy witnesses this time and no incriminating evidence left behind.

The crater which the blast opened up was never completely filled because the men in the blasting party didn't dare stay in the vicinity too long. Anyhow, they thought, if a big enough hole remained, at least there could be no doubt that the mortal remains of Sir Craigie had truly been removed.

Back at the tavern that night, most of the conspirators felt quite good about the adventure. They had tackled an impossible job and accomplished it gloriously. But Uncle Yankee, who besides his other interesting weaknesses had an incurable addiction to fine horses, didn't share the elation of the others. Instead he ordered an extra drink or two to assuage his grief. "No matter whether that stud was Protestant, Catholic, or Conservative," he said, "that sure was one hell of a going-out. And the Lord will like as not hold me responsible for it someday."

Many years later, and after he had given the villagers many another sacrilege to chuckle about, came a day when my uncle had to choose between the two rival cemeteries for his own burial. The doctor had been summoned that morning when Yankee couldn't get up to start the fire and after gravely working over the sick man with his mysterious tools, he suddenly began to look out at the sky as if a hole might be opening in it.

"Guess I better get ready to pass in my checks, eh Doc?"

"Not a bad idea, Yankee."

"How long do you give me?"

"A week, maybe. Maybe less."

There was the usual tight pause and the usual nervous shufflings on the other side of the bedroom door.

"The wife's going to be upset some," Yankee said. "If you've got time, Doc, maybe you'd break it to her before you go."

My aunt was Irish Catholic and so devout that there was as much terror as grief in her reaction. Her beloved husband was going to die outside of the Faith. Lost . . . . It was the one terrible fear of her life come true at last. For nearly fifty years now she had been tearfully lighting votive candles for her persistently carefree husband, praying that she might be able to point him to the One True Light before it was too late. And now the awful time was come and Yankee still wasn't prepared; there would be nothing more than the Anglican minister to go with him to the Protestant cemetery, there to read a text or two about heaven over him as if he didn't know damn well that Yankee had no more chance of getting there than Sir Craigie had had. It was quite enough to move the poor woman to the point of hysteria.

"Ah please woman don't carry on so!" Yankee begged.

"But — but Daddy you must be so scared!"

"Scared?" Yankee repeated reaching for her hand. "Sure and I've forgot how to be scared, Mama. Forgot how when I married you!" And he asked one of his boys if they couldn't somehow manage a drink to put a little bottom in her.

By nightfall however, when it became painfully clear that neither words nor whiskey could bring my aunt any comfort, my uncle called on one of his boys to discuss a more desperate strategy.

"Never figured I'd go out crawlin' " he said, "but if you think the priest would come up to see me, maybe you'd better get him. I can't stand any more of your mother's cryin'."

So it was that the very last of my uncle's lifetime of doing the unexpected was to become a Catholic on his death bed. And the Anglican padre, who had been quietly alerted the day before, was told now that he wouldn't have to bother after all. That the priest would take Yankee out to the R.C. cemetery with all the rights and privileges pertaining thereto.

Thirty years later my good friend Cornelius Callaghan told me that, as the undertaker in charge of the funeral, he had been called upon to make a rather unexpected defense of Yankee's remarkable conversion. This defense, as one might suspect, had to be made to a doubting Protestant — an especially upright and quietly godly old Presbyterian by the name of Billy Oakes.

"Maybe you'll mind now that at the time Billy was helping to look after the cemeteries — digging graves included — and we were on our way out to the cemetery this day see, to get your uncle's grave ready, see . . . . The roads were so bad just then that we couldn't use a truck, so here we are the two of us with the lend of Letty Raymond's old horse and Yankee's rough box in the wagon behind and — well I could see that Billy was doing quite a bit of thinking about your uncle checkin' in, and I thought maybe at first it was just because he'd lived almost next door to Yankee most of his life. And then all at once he says to me, 'Look Callaghan, I don't want you to think I'm tryin' to make fun of you Micks or anything like that, but do you really think Yankee can get past the Pearly Gates just by callin' in a priest when it's almost time to pass over? I mean — well, you know the hell-raisin' he did all his life. Just didn't give a hoot for anything or anybody. . . . Come on now Callaghan. Try to be honest for once even if you are a Mick and tell me if you don't think a conversion like Yankee's isn't just a mite too convenient?' "

Cornelius assures me that he answerd the question by referring to the Good Book itself. "You remember how it was with
Our Lord when He was being crucified," he began. "How Our
Lord turned to the thief who had just repented of his sins as he
hung on the cross and promised him that "this day thou shalt be
with me in Paradise." "Yes," Callaghan concluded, "I must say
I'll have to go along with the priest on this. I think Yankee's
made it safe home all right. . . ."

But Cornelius tells me that something still seemed to be bothering Billy, that the reins got slack in his hands and he began to
shake his head.

"Well," Cornelius told him, "I didn't really expect to convince
you, Billy. It takes more time than that to christianize a Presbyterian, you know."

"Oh it's not that I don't believe you really. Not that at all,
Cornelius."

"Well then how come you keep shaking your head?"

Billy looked off over the horse's ears and way beyond, and
Cornelius tells me that a sad kind of smile came over him. "I
guess," he said quietly, "I was just thinkin' about all that I've
been missing all these years and probably didn't have to at all."

Chapter Three

❖❖❖❖❖❖❖❖❖❖❖❖❖❖❖❖❖❖❖❖❖❖❖❖❖

Since the haphazard contemplations of this book have already wandered onto the subject of horse funerals, this might be as good a time as any to tell you about the sad end of Letty Raymond's horse — the dispirited nag we saw transporting my uncle's rough-box and the two philosophers of the last chapter.

There was still a place for the horse in the small town of forty years ago. First of all, there was generally an adequate place to board him because one of the inalienable rights of village living in those days was that every house could use the space which belonged to it in any way that the owner fancied. And at the back of that independent little piece of earth there usually sat a small shingled barn which in the beginning had probably been designed to shelter a milk cow, a pen of pigs, a pair of geese, a couple of dozen hens and a horse. The family cow began to disappear in the '20's. (My father started the first milk route in Arthur in 1921.) And for those families which began to acquire social aspirations, the pigs were next to go. Though it was admittedly very cosy to have a barrel of your own pork and sausage frozen out in the woodshed to start the winter, there was something distinctly lowbrow about "sloppin' pigs." It was something you'd expect the Irish to do, perhaps, or some old man just moved in from the country. Pigs smelled, broke out and rooted everything rootable. Butchering too was a disgustingly common thing to have to do in your own garden with all the neighbours gawking and giving advice and trying to dodge the blood gushes as the poor animal ran itself dry of life. Then there was the awful mess of guts and lungs and the little brats fighting for the bladder so they could empty out the urine and blow it into a football while it was still warm and rubbery.

So pigs were among the first casualties of the rising standard of living, and if the new progress was so determined that nothing could stop it, the rest of the livestock disappeared from that shingled barn too, in which case its only function was to conceal the backhouse which invariably hid on the far side of it under an astonishingly luxuriant growth of wild cucumbers and holly-hocks. But in many of the village barns which were familiar to me as a boy, the hens and the horse were still there. The hens in fact have never disappeared; and now with the horse coming back from oblivion in the role of a playmate, rather than as a beast of burden, the hometown barns are again becoming almost as useful as they were intended to be.

When I was a lad of ten or twelve however, it was not ex-actly easy for the horse to survive the onslaught of the Model-T and all the noisy machines which came with it. But one could manage a much larger garden or potato plot if one had a horse to hitch to a plow in May and a scuffler in July. And that same horse was equally useful for an unpredictable variety of hauling jobs, most important of which was the bringing of the winter's fuel supply from the bush.

With a horse in the stable, a man simply had that added mea-sure of independence which has always rewarded the possessor of power. To Letty Raymond, however, his steed was hardly a mark of prestige, for Letty was one of the humbler citizens of the village and so poor that he sometimes didn't have enough to eat. He lived at the edge of town in a tarpapered shack with an Irish wife who seemed remarkably fat for all their lack of gro-ceries, and he was that versatile kind of workman we commonly referred to as "a jackass of all trades." But his chief asset in making his precarious livelihood was his horse. Sometimes the poor brute merely took Letty and his tools to his job. More often the horse was the one who had to do the work when they arrived, for to him fell such jobs as cartage, cultivating, mowing roadside weeds, hauling garbage for the families who had no pigs, drawing cordwood, and in the winter, plowing the side-walks free of snow.

Now it would make a far prettier story if I could tell you that Letty's horse was well paid for all his sweat and strain. He wasn't. Not that Letty abused his horse with the whip as was so often the case in those days. Nor did he hurry him with threats and swear words. Usually it was the successful, fast-moving men who were roughest on their horses. Letty was hardly impatient enough or energetic enough to be really cruel to an animal.

But he wasn't energetic enough to put away much hay for the winter either, and as a result the horse was pitifully thin by the time the grass began to shine again in the spring.

"Why in the world doesn't Letty feed that horse a few oats!" my father used to say as we would see the poor brute struggling with its task for the day. And I remember that once when Letty had done some little chore for us, father gave him a bag of oats along with his pay. "They aren't the best," he explained, "but maybe your horse won't be too particular."

Came an April morning when Letty went out to the barn and found that his horse wouldn't try to get up. He coaxed, patted, lifted and threw down a forkful of hay with daisies in it, but the horse seemed to have no interest in the things of this world at all. Alarmed now, Letty ran into the house and got a bowl of rolled oats from the oatmeal bag, but even with this bait in front of his nose, the poor brute made only the feeblest effort to get to his feet.

Letty never thought too clearly in an emergency and by the time he got back to the house to report to his wife, he was crying.

"Well go down and get the vet!" Bridget told him. "Get, now!"

So ten minutes later Letty was explaining his predicament to the grizzled old veterinarian who kept a dispensary near the foot of Main street. "I have no money to pay you, doc," Letty said, "but there might be some diggin' I could do for you sometime."

The vet listened with full professional decorum and then went out to his stable where he uncovered an old canvas sling. "Tell you what," he said, "I haven't had any oats myself this morning yet, but how be you get this sling under his belly and see if you can get him hoisted to his feet and I'll be there to give him the once-over as soon as I've had my breakfast."

By the time my cousin and I happened by the place that morning on our way to school the sling had been worked under the animal's discouraged belly, and the two ends were looped over the hook of a block and tackle which had been slung from the peak of the rafters. "You lads are just in time!" Letty told us. "Get hold of that there rope now!"

The horse should have realized that he couldn't hope to die in peace with a crew like us, who were now determined to resurrect him. At his head was the biggest man in our end of town, a good-natured moron who had long ago despaired of his more civilized name and was known simply as "Duckfoot Bill." At the wizened rear of the patient, getting ready to use the tail as a handle, was Letty himself. The rest of us were braced tug-of-war fashion outside on the long rope which threaded through the block and tackle.

"Get ready!" Letty hollered. "Ho! Heave!"

We of the rope dug our heels in the mud and pulled, while Letty put the tail over his shoulder and tried to stand up with it, and up front Duckfoot Bill grunted mightily. The pulleys creaked and the rafters spat dust and slowly the old canvas sling began to lift its sorry burden clear of the floor. Then suddenly came the ominous sound of ripping. Letty held up his hand and the horse's bulk sank slowly to the floor again.

"Was that his tail comin' out?" Duckfoot Bill wanted to know.

"Jesus Whiz!" Letty moaned surveying the damage. "There's the Doc's sling all shot to hell. . . . Well Bridget, what do we do now?"

But Bridget's advice, whatever it was, didn't matter much because just about then the horse began to quiver and kick in the most awesome manner and in spite of the cup of perfectly good whisky a neighbour poured down his throat, he was dead a half hour later.

Letty's eyes were red and his face streaked with tears again when the veterinarian finally arrived. "I tell you Doc, I never saw a horse die like that in all my life! What do you suppose happened to him anyhow?"

In his most professional bedside manner, the good doctor listened carefully as Letty detailed all of the symptoms. "And what did you feed him, Letty?" he asked.

"I fed him all I could, Doc. Fed him everything I had!"

The other man picked up his black bag then and his tattered sling and made what must surely have been one of the kindliest diagnosis in all veterinary history. "Off-hand, and just from what you've told me, Letty," he said, "I'd say he died from fat around the heart."

Chapter Four

❖❖❖❖❖❖❖❖❖❖❖❖❖❖❖❖❖❖❖❖❖❖❖❖❖❖

Also at the head of Main Street, though discreetly with-drawn from its dust and noisy interest, was the school, scowling through the gloom of maple shadows. It was a two-storey brick building capped with a bell tower and behind it was an acre of grassy playground. It had three classrooms and two playrooms. In my day we sat two to a bench, wrote on blackboards made of painted plaster, and tripped over plank floors which had with-stood so many generations of boots before ours that the knots stood a half-inch higher than the rest of the wood. Up front the teacher reigned from a foot-high platform which emphasized his absolute power and gave him a fearsome mechanical advantage when it came time to wield the strap.

It was the New England historian Henry Adams who once declared that "no man can be a schoolmaster for ten years and remain fit for anything else." (He was a lifelong teacher himself and his wife committed suicide.)

Adams wouldn't have been surprised, then, at the barbarism which was common to the school which whacked me along the unroyal road to learning, for in the old hometown it was the tra-dition for teachers to take root and live forever.

Which isn't to say that these everlasting teachers had no ene-mies in town. Most of them had plenty of enemies, and for a hundred good reasons. Some were so neurotic they must have made neurotics of many of their pupils as well. Some were sim-ply tyrants who acted as though they had a divine right to terrify, and what little teaching they attempted seemed just another means to that end. Still others were outright sadists. I shall never forget the glow of Satanic ecstasy which used to flush the face of one of those teachers as the strap would be brought whistling down onto the palms of some poor little sinner — brought down

35

time and time again, until the child's hands would be swelled like a grapefruit for the rest of the day.

"There now! Maybe that will cure you of being stupid for awhile!"

Sometimes a parent would come storming down the road ready to strip the hide from a teacher and hang it up to dry behind the nearest backhouse. Sometimes the town constable had to be called in to prevent mayhem. Sometimes the reeve was asked to intercede. In fact, teacher could make himself so unpopular that he could precipitate a full-sized feud on election day. But neither the threat of fists, nor intercessions by the reeve, nor even a school board election could ever seem to dislodge a teacher once his roots had twisted deeply enough into the community soil. For then, as now, schooling was regarded as something so mysteriously sacred and untouchable that firing a teacher was almost as unthinkable as defrocking a priest.

The building itself was quite as crude as the men and women who were in charge of it. It had no electricity, no running water, no flush toilets. Aside from a few prints of the Royal Family, there were no pictures to break the monotony of the kalsomined walls, and it was a frivolous teacher indeed who permitted the pupils to decorate a classroom. In the basement, a temperamental furnace burned either wood or coal, according to the whim of the trustees; and sometimes when the wind was from the east the smoke would billow up from the registers so thick that we would have to hoist the windows to let it out.

To learn is to suffer, so the Greeks used to say, and that gospel is still fiercely championed by certain thick-skinned individuals with intellectual pretensions, particularly those who can brag of the birchings they used to absorb at some exclusive English school. And to tell the truth, that penitentiary atmosphere did contribute to my learning, though hardly in the manner the discipline-minded critics would suspect. It was our teachers' peculiar attitude towards books which really made an educated man of me. There was no library in the old school, not a bookshelf anywhere. We had our text books, didn't we? And judging by how stupid we were at mastering the simple things that were in our few texts, wasn't it more than obvious that we had no business dilly-dallying into books that weren't even on the course? Besides, when a child got the idea to strike out on his own with reading, there was no telling what kind of lewd stuff he might become addicted to, was there?

So reading then, except for what we were told to read, was usually forbidden. Oh there were a few tattered volumes on the front of the teacher's desk and, if one was a very good little pupil who finished his exercise way ahead of the rest, one might, as a very special favour, be loaned a book from the teacher's own private stock. But reading as a reward was a very rare privilege indeed, something generally reserved for the clean, smart kids from Crown Hill — the kids who never got the strap either.

But in all the world there is no lure more enticing than the lure of the forbidden, and that was why so many of us stubborn, backward brats from the tile-yard end of town got into the habit of reading just for the hell of it. By sneaking out a book as one might sneak a cigarette, and doing it so often that the sin became incurable.

Sometimes the forbidden book was one which had been bootlegged from somebody's home. (Grandparents from Scotland always seemed to have brought books with them.) Sometimes it was a title from the dingy little library downtown that was open every Tuesday evening. Sometimes, if someone was in the mood to prove himself a hero, one of the books on the teacher's desk might be lifted. One kind of literature which was always available to underground readers those days was the Wild West magazine which our big brothers bought in the drug store for a dime and then traded till it fell apart. And of all the acts of bravery a lad could manage then, none was more gloriously reckless than that of soberly standing your big geography text upright on your desk, as if you had finally decided to learn something from it, when you were only using it as a shield for the dime novel flat on your desk in front of you.

There was a second reason why the cast-iron discipline of my old school contributed greatly to my learning, and I doubt if the critics will understand that either.

To any but the poor fellow who was crushed into total surrender, there were times when the combination of scowling, stomping, shaming, shouting and strapping was just too much to endure. And at such times we might simply hide our books in a hollow tree or a dry culvert and discover the world in whatever way seemed in keeping with the weather.

Come a soft blue and gold day in autumn and there would be so many things to study out of doors it is a wonder we ever went to school at all. Winter, however, was not so good for hookey-players because there were so few places one could go. The livery stable was warm and it had a beautiful smell, but there was always the danger that the hotel-keeper would find you and turn you over to the principal, particularly if there were enough of you to raise a rumpus. The grist mill was too cold and the smart-alecks down at the saw mill would be sure to put you to work. But if you were the kind who didn't mind playing hookey with nothing but a book for company, there were all sorts of nooks to be found, many of them in the school itself. One could lock himself in a toilet for instance, or sneak up into the attic, or pick the lock of the equipment cubicle down in the boys' playroom — the place where they stored broken desks and the Boer War uniforms we wore on cadet inspection day. The retreat which I liked best was the coal-bin down cellar.

Very often nothing was said next day about such an absence. Teachers have always been fortunately unobservant, and even if a lad did have to pay for his day of peace, he was usually so accustomed to the strap by then that the punishment didn't matter too much.

It is with regret that I must warn those parents who may be considering a move from the city that the tradition of hookey-playing seems to have pretty well disappeared in the country, and that the average school with its incredibly expensive new building and its sparkling new equipment and its bright new breed of teachers, scientifically directing every pupil's every step, is probably no improvement at all now over the education factory you have right where you are.

One of these days we are going to wake up to the fact that the learning which makes a better citizen and a happier man is not going to be mass-produced through the gadgetry of modern communication, more degrees for more teachers, and more equipment than our money can buy.

The only really important responsibility of any school, as I see it, is simply to turn out pupils who burn to read; but for all

our modern technology and our eager, specially-trained peda-
gogues we are apparently as far as ever from discovering any
certain way of accomplishing this. But here was our old school
making book-lovers of us in spite of all its determination to the
contrary, and without it costing the taxpayer one cent! All it had
to do was to make schooling so utterly intolerable that we became a generation of hookey-players, and to make reading for
pleasure something exquisitely rare and forbidden. Something to
be bought only through defiant adventure and to be paid for,
upon demand, with two handfuls of welts duly received in front
of the class.

Is it any wonder that a love of reading so hard-bought as ours
would never leave us? That it would survive even the dreary
years of literature lessons which were to be inflicted upon us till
the last of our certificates were folded into the Family Bible?

Speaking of this business of teaching literature, I wonder if
today's pupil is really getting any better break than I did forty-
five years ago. I had the sad privilege of witnessing a demonstra-
tion lesson in the teaching of English Literature the other day. It
was at a teachers' convention and for forty minutes I watched a
scholarly gentleman labour with a class of senior high school
students on "The Symbolism in Charles Dickens' *Great Expec-
tations.*"

Now, of all the authors which today's students have to meet,
I had always supposed that Dickens was surely one man whose
writing was so direct and uncomplicated that a teacher couldn't
spoil it for a class even if he tried. But though I have enjoyed
feuding with teachers ever since I was a first-grader with a hand
the same width as the strap, it seems that I had forgotten how
skilful a really zealous pedagogue can be at prescribing the max-
imum of labour to bring forth the minimum of mouse.

And I listened with dismay as this hard-working teacher delv-
ed into that novel as Sherlock Holmes might have done, sleuth-
ing passage after passage for secondary meanings and other
mysterious profundities. By the end of the lesson, one was almost convinced that Dickens had buried these tidbits throughout
the book in much the same way that a Cubmaster might have
hidden the clues to a game of Scavenger Hunt.

When Dickens begins this novel by reading the family name of his lead character from his parents' tombstone, it wasn't to get the spelling right after all, it seems, but to symbolize impending doom. Nor was the beacon mentioned on the following page included in the description of the shoreline merely because it was a characteristic fixture for such a locality — Dickens intended it to symbolize the beam of hope which is always beckoning the lost safe home if they will only heed. Ivy, growing up over mounds of ruin, wasn't mentioned by the author merely to balance out the colour of the picture he is describing — it is there to symbolize the ultimate in decay and forgotten sorrows. And when, in the final paragraph of the novel, Dickens tells us simply that "the evening mists were rising now," he wasn't talking about the weather at all. It was merely a symbolic way to let the reader know that all the survivors inthe novel will live happily ever after.

The teacher ended the lesson on a note of regret that time should now put an end to so fascinating a study, but he compensated to the best of his ability by assigning for homework a half-dozen other places in the book where a diligent student might find delightful examples of the same kind of literary genius.

As for me, I got up from the lesson with two principal regrets. Firstly, that Dickens couldn't have been present to defend himself; and secondly, that in this age when the average teacher is undoubtedly a much more enlightened individual than his predecessor was, there should still be such a dutiful determination to make reading into something to be sweated over.

I have already confessed that I cherish an unreasonable prejudice against the teaching profession, so you will discount my comments accordingly.

But as I look back over my school years now, it seems that I was made to endure a long and dreary procession of teachers who, like Saint Paul, seem to have been religiously persuaded that any human pursuit which was pleasurable was of necessity worldly and worthy of instant crucifixion. Pupils weren't in school to be entertained. Most certainly not. And reading hadn't been placed on the curriculum for the sake of enjoyment. Now that we were come to the place where we should put away childish things, our reading now had to be broken up into the examination subjects of literature, grammar and composition. We had to spend hours dissecting rhyme schemes, breaking lines of immortal beauty into poetic feet, memorizing the proper definitions for such things as a metaphor, a bare predicate, alliteration, personification and a host of other literary labels which might be required of us on "the final."

From the more memorable prose passages, our teachers selected an infinite variety of sentences for grammatical analysis. Under penalty of the hickory, we were warned that a preposition was one part of speech we should never end a sentence with. And similarly we must, under no condition, ever begin a sentence with "and." We filled our notebooks with rules such as these and did our best to remember them all when, after the last line of some major selection had been painfully masticated, we were forced to write a three-hundred word essay on why we considered the piece great literature.

For that one redeeming feature in that old school of mine which I have already mentioned, down in the basement, under the cobwebs back of the furnace, there was that coal-bin which none of my teachers ever seems to have explored. It was dark down there, but unless a storm had piled too much snow against the solitary window, there was always light enough to read by. And it was in that lovely old coal-bin, safe from the ministrations and discipline of the teacher, that I was able to discover reading as a pastime — the most wonderful pastime in all the world. It is a love which has deepened with every passing year, and for that love I shall be eternally grateful to that coal-bin. To my teachers, however, I feel that I owe nothing but Christian forgiveness.

This is not to lament the passing of the coal-bin. It is instead a protest that in this era of pedagogical enlightenment, when our teachers are finally being paid enough to know better, so many of our youngsters are being led to hate books.

Why doesn't Johnny read? Why does his older brother come home on the day he quits school to toss his literature books into the attic with an oath never to look at them again? I think there can be only one answer. Instead of being shown that the only important purpose of reading is for enjoyment, he has been forced into being a critic, a dissector, a grammarian, and above all, a passer of examinations.

He hasn't been permitted to merely absorb the obvious, even when the author intended him to do so. All too frequently the class motto has been "Think! There must be a harder way!" And his teachers have gone on, year after year, incessantly plowing up the gentlest of literary landscapes for supposed hidden meanings, much as a sow might root for truffles.

It is high time surely for some one of us book-lovers to come down off the fence with a stick in his hand and demand that such depredations come to an end. Neither the author nor the bewildered pupil deserves to endure them any longer.

Chapter Five

❖❖❖❖❖❖❖❖❖❖❖❖❖❖❖❖❖❖❖❖❖❖❖

I see that down in New Brunswick the other day a pupil graduated from High School the hard way — by refusing to take the strap. Or perhaps it would be more accurate to say that he took the strap more literally than was proper. He took it right out of the principal's hand and lambasted that scholarly gentleman around the office a few times before he took off for the woods.

It seems to me that pupils aren't quite as subtle as they used to be about doing battle with an unpopular teacher. In all my life I never did belt a teacher, though I certainly suffered under some who deserved it. I was never quite brave enough or big enough I guess, and anyhow there were much more interesting and safer ways to even the score. I well remember a certain Hallowe'en in our town for instance when a freshly sacrificed skunk found its way into a teacher's desk. I also recall the morning when one of our snippy, uppity young schoolmarms just fresh from the city found a nestful of squirming pink mice in one of her galoshes.

But of all the pranks that were traditional to schoolboys then, none was quite so appropriate I think as the "bean treatment." For those who have never had to run the gauntlet of a country school it should be explained that the "bean treatment" was not only one of the most dramatic of all pupil revenges but something which was quite educational as well.

First you needed an empty chalk box, one of the wooden type with a slide top that used to sit on every teacher's desk in the land a couple of generations ago. Next you had to get some sawdust. There was always some left over from the packing around the chalk sticks, and in those days it was a very simple matter to get as much more as you needed from the nearest woodpile. The active ingredient in the formula was a cupful of beans. The big, speckled beans from your old man's stock of garden seeds were best, and after you had mixed beans and sawdust in sufficient quantity to fill the chalk box tightly you went out to the pump and got a half a dipper of water and wet the mixture thoroughly. If you could hardly slide the lid back on you knew that you had done the job to perfection.

Once the lid was driven home you set the box back on the teacher's desk where it had been before you started monkeying with it, and there it sat for three or four days, or longer, looking just as innocent as you did. But finally came the breathless morning when the unsuspecting schoolmarm came in to her day's work and found the box split in all four directions, with sawdust and bean sprouts all over the place.

"Who did it? Come on now! Who was the smart one this time?"

She would learn, if she taught long enough in a country school, that there was at least one thing we feared even more than a fearsome teacher and that was to be labelled a tattler. She could keep us in till dark and we still wouldn't tell. I don't remember now whether that snippity, uppity, little witch kept us in the time we performed the experiment for her or not. Come to think of it, I can remember very few of her lessons either. But the results of that germinating box of beans were so spectacular that I never could forget the beautiful irrepressibility of growing things — that you simply cannot contain the surge of bursting new life.

Which was one lesson that our teacher never did learn. She just tried harder than ever to keep the lid on us.

Chapter Six

❖❖❖❖❖❖❖❖❖❖❖❖❖❖❖❖❖❖❖❖❖❖❖❖❖❖

It is getting near to Father's Day again as I write this, and
yesterday I was shopping around for a card. I have never seen
such a variety of cards as there is this year, nor did I ever suspect that there could be so many jokes made about this business
of fatherhood. Some of these witty cards were a half a yard high.
There were plenty of sentimental cards too, and in some of these
the poetry was quite fresh and beautiful. But try as I might, I
couldn't seem to find anything which was even remotely in keeping with the particular memory which was in my mind at the
time.

Which wasn't surprising really because that particular memory of my father was centered about one of the humblest, most
unromantic possessions a man can have.

You see, Father's Day also happens to be very near to school-
ending time, and while our parents rarely gave us children gifts
at any time but Christmas, this was the momentous year when I
was finally saying goodbye to the battered old, hickory-swinging
Public School. In those days that wonderful rite of passing out
of Public School in Ontario was called "getting our entrance"
and since this was undoubtedly the biggest accomplishment a lad
could then achieve, I had been hinting for some time now that I
really should be honoured with some kind of tangible recogni-
tion. There was a lovely pitcher's mitt down in Henry's Hardware, for instance, for only $3.25.

Well, in all justice to my parents, I must confess that they
gave me ample warning. "No," they told me, "we don't have
money for that kind of spending."

But I kept thinking that maybe, maybe, on that last day of
school, my father and mother would somehow find a way to buy
me a graduation present. And surely enough, on that very day

of the final examination, when my father came home after delivering the milk, there was a store-wrapped box in the wagon. The box, by the feel of it, was cardboard, about fourteen inches long and six across, and whatever was inside it didn't rattle. I thought I knew what it was and I was utterly delighted.

"Oh I bet I can guess what's in that!" I said when my father brought it in. "It's leather, isn't it?"

"Yes," he said quietly. "Leather, all right."

"And it cost about three dollars too, didn't it?"

That figure didn't seem to be too far out either. Then, right before my eyes, the delicious dream was shattered as my father ripped off the paper to reveal a common shoebox. And inside was a pair of boots — work-boots for himself.

A half-hour later my mother found me upstairs crying, and when I looked up I was surprised to see that she was holding, not the new pair of boots, but the old ones they had replaced.

"I want you to look at them!" she said. "Look at what's left of them. Look at the heels! And the holes in the soles and the way the toe is ready to lift like a cover . . . . Have you any idea of how far those boots have travelled — just to keep us fed, and warm and together . . . ?"

I didn't answer, but I did know, as every farm boy knew in those days, that to plow one lonely acre of land then meant ten miles of walking behind a team and a single furrow plow.

"Would you really have enjoyed that pitcher's glove if it meant that your dad had to keep on plowing in boots like these?" she asked.

And then she put the twisted, battered, stone-bruised boots down on the floor beside my bed and quietly closed the door behind her.

And when I finally decided to go downstairs again and out into the day, there was a maturity suddenly come upon me that had nothing at all to do with my being proud of finishing public school.

Chapter Seven

❖❖❖❖❖❖❖❖❖❖❖❖❖❖❖❖❖❖❖❖❖❖❖❖❖

Speaking of Henry's Hardware a moment ago, I was reminded of how eagerly we youngsters used to await the great day when that store would receive its annual shipment of bamboo poles. For when these were displayed outside on the sidewalk beside the flats of petunias and tomato plants, it was the final proof that spring was really come and that it was time to go fishing.

Now there was a rumour that down in Toronto, where they had a set of Parliament buildings of some sort, there was a Department of Game and Fisheries which laid down some pretty hard-and-fast rules about fishing, including an opening date that didn't make any sense at all. But Toronto was at least seventy miles away and we did our best not to support the place with any of our tax-money, so we didn't think any government, way down there, had any moral right to interfere with our fishing. So the season opened when Henry's Hardware got its annual bundle of bamboo rods. A quarter apiece they were for the best of them, and I recall my father hanging onto that quarter as if it had grown to his palm.

"Now why in the world do you have to have one of these high-fallutin' poles all the way from China?" he would ask. "Just because they cost money? Why couldn't you just go out to some willow and cut yourself a nice smooth limb? That's what I used to do when I was a lad."

But I generally got the quarter eventually and sometimes if you could catch the old man in a really expansive mood — after you'd cleaned a couple of pig pens for him, maybe — you could also work him for one of these gaily coloured floats which told you when you had a nice fat chub just itching to get hauled ashore. They cost 15 cents, and that, plus 2 cents worth of

47

hooks and some fishing line left over from last year, constituted as complete a set of fishing gear as a boy could hope for. Or a man either.

I went into that same old store when I was back home last spring — it goes by another name now but it smells the same — and do you think I could find a bamboo pole? Not for 25 cents or any other price.

"How come?" I asked. "Do we hate China *that* much?"

The smart young clerk assured me that our international politics had nothing to do with it. "It's just that there's no more demand for that kind of pole," he said. They had fishing rods though, dozens of them — nylon, fibreglass, split cane, razor-blade steel — anything you could think of *but* bamboo. And each with a reel mounted on the handle. Precision made, 17-jewel reels that were a sheer joy to hold in the hand. Pretty proud equipment indeed for a community where the creek is rarely more than two frog-hops wide.

Apparently you're not supposed to simply get excited now and yank the fish out of the water with a worm and a yell. You must have the proper technique and the proper equipment today. So you *reel* the fish in, and the assortment of hooks, flies, lures, pickled polliwogs and what-not, which is standard equipment now, is so extensive that you have to have a special tackle box to hold it. Open it up and it looks like a fruit salad.

I see that some fishermen still use worms however, but do they dig for them over on the other side of the manure pile like they used to? Not bloody likely, as Noel Coward would say. For it seems only a matter of time now before the humble, home-dug dew-worm will be a part of ancient history because I see in today's paper that down in the States they are now selling worms in automatic vending machines. Half-a-dollar a dozen is the price the machine demands, and one machine which was especially refrigerated and decked out in flashing neon lights is reported to have sold over three thousand worms in a single weekend.

Makes me feel related to one of these bearded, way-out, guitar-strumming hippies who, in a Montreal night-club the other night, told us, "It sure is a crazy world, and I'm glad I'm not in it!"

Chapter Eight

�֍✤✤✤✤✤✤✤✤✤✤✤✤✤✤✤✤✤✤✤✤✤✤✤✤✤

In his book *Wolf Willow* Wallace Stegner remembers the small town of his boyhood as an unpleasantly brutal place where the heroes were tough, pain-shrugging men who could lick anything their fists could reach. But Stegner grew up in Saskatchewan at a time when that country was still so untamed that only brute strength and endurance dared challenge it. I must confess, however, that life in any small town does give a lad more opportunity to be a young barbarian. In my day we trapped, hunted, speared and snared, and we had no particular conscience about the suffering we caused. We blew up bullfrogs with a goose-quill and laughed when they tried to dive. We might cure a dog that wouldn't stay home by tying cans to his tail or rubbing his rectum with turpentine. And we were all fighters.

A few years ago my old friend Jim Hamilton had an item in the hometown weekly which must have provoked many a wistful smile from those of us who no longer boast of our birthdays. The item merely announces that an old church shed which Jim and I both knew very well has now entirely disappeared. It reads:

> *Removal of the last foundation stones of the Arthur United Church shed was made earlier this month and a tacit reminder of a bygone era is no more. Many recall when the old shed served as a place of rest for weary horses while their masters did business in Arthur stores or discussed local and world affairs on a street corner. The building itself was taken down several years ago, its timbers sold and part of the foundation used in the erection of the gates at the fair grounds. Undoubtedly an improvement has been made in*

the appearance of this part of town but demolition of the
old wall has awakened some long, long memories in the
minds of district oldtimers.

I'm willing to bet that the memories Jim had in the back of
his mind when he wrote that had very little to do with the church
or even church people. Because I happened to have been an old
schoolmate of Jim's, and I recall as if it were yesterday that this
same church shed was sort of boys' club for the whole town.
More specifically, it was the accepted place for the fist-fights
which in those days seemed to be an inescapable part of a
youngster's extra-curricular education.

You would be playing hockey in the school yard, for instance,
and suddenly you would find yourself, stick at the ready, squar-
ing off with some lad on the other team who was determined to
spill blood. But no sooner had the first blow landed when both
of you would find yourselves in the grip of the older boys.

"Want to fight, boys? O.K." they would say, "that's just jake-
a-loo! Only don't waste a good fight on the school grounds, eh?
You'd only get whaled for it afterward anyhow . . . ."

And so, before you could do anything about it, you would
find yourselves taken over body and soul by managers. It was
often rather frightening to find yourself so suddenly famous, because now, what might have been a private little tiff was the
talk of the whole school — the male half, anyhow. And that
evening after four o'clock, as sure as God put worms in apples,
you would be a gladiator in the Methodist Church shed, fighting
to your last ounce of strength while a half-hundred of your
bloodthirsty schoolmates cheered or jeered.

Gloves? Yes, we fought with gloves, but these were never the
official over-stuffed variety you may find now in any Y.M.C.A.
They were just the leather work gloves, lent to us for the occasion by a couple of the bigger boys, and when one landed on
your nose the smell of the stable was often mixed in with the
pain.

So you whaled away, you ducked, whaled again and wondered, with the taste of blood in your mouth, whether you should
quit or be noble and wait till you were knocked down into the
manure of the ring.

But such behaviour doesn't prove that there was something about village life which made us basically cruel and insensitive. It was merely one of the less fortunate results of a way of life in which a boy was allowed to grow up with an absolute minimum of adult supervision. There were no playground managers or Lions' Clubs or Scoutmasters to take charge of his leisure in those days. Every lad had a certain amount of work to do of course, either for his own family or for someone else, but once that duty was accomplished he was again the captain of his soul. And while this traditional lack of direction made life pretty miserable for a mama's boy and for some of the dogs, groundhogs and bullfrogs of the community, it did encourage a kind of resourcefulness and independence that is regrettably beyond the reach of the modern urban youngster.

And I am glad to say that this is one aspect of life in the country or country village which the years have been unable to change very much. Give a boy the freedom and the raw materials which are still to be found wherever unsupervised space is found and it will humble you a little to discover how little he needs you. Or how much more he will learn when you can't get your hands on him to bring him up properly.

I am thinking right now of that unique establishment at our farm known to the boys as "The Clubhouse." It is a six-by-eight cubicle built on top of the pig pen and it has all of the attributes which a secret rendezvous for boys must have. It is inaccessible to all but the very brave, for its solitary window cannot be opened and the only entrance is through a trap door in the floor. From this door a rope ladder is let down to those visitors who have the password. But even blood-members have to first brave the attentions of a very husky pen of pigs, one of which has the annoying habit of persistently nudging from behind any climber who attempts to swing himself up the ladder.

In short, the hideout is absolutely girl-proof and almost mother-proof. Females with a complaint or a plea to utter, stand without the outer gates and try to make themselves heard above the complaints and pleas of the pigs.

The labour on this unique club, has been done by the boys themselves, and whatever flaws there may have been in the internal construction has been pretty well camouflaged by the shingling on the outside. That these shingles come in several different colours and shapes, does not seem to bother the builders at all. They assure me that the first rain revealed but a single small leak which a piece of bubble gum soon repaired.

A lantern hangs on a spike at one peak, and a sheep-skin serves as a couch. An orange crate is bookcase to some half-hundred comic books, and there are sundry other valuables such as a cheap pair of field-glasses, a bird guide, some clam shells, half a deer horn, and an old air rifle which they have been trying to repair for at least a year now.

But what intrigues me most about the little fortress is its interior decoration, for the inside has been lined from top to bottom with pictures. Needless to say, these serve as insulating material as well, hence the preference of those with heavy cardboard backing.

But it struck me rather odd at first, that whenever the dimension to be filled required it, the picture was simply turned on its side. The effect of such a mural, with some of the pictures standing upright, and others reclining on their backs, just didn't seem to be in keeping with the taste and care with which the decorators had designed the place, and I told them so.

"So what," came the reply. "They look just as good one way as the other. Some pictures you lay down to see right, and others you don't! So what's wrong with that?"

Which was a pretty good question, come to think of it, and one which is apt to take an oldster back a long, long way to the days when all that one had to do to get a fresh and more interesting view of the world was to bend one's head down as far as a supple little spine would allow and then look back between your legs at it.

But we were soon broken of that ungraceful habit along with a lot of other rather delightful freedoms. We were taught the stern meaning of order — that the top was meant to be up and the bottom neatly beneath it. And the discipline of schools took some twelve years of our lives and a lot of the taxpayers' money and effort to make sure that our conforming was complete.

So we conform now, and every year of our hidebound lives we spend more and more money to become more and more proper. It is a genuine mark of culture now to be genuinely hard to please, and keeping a home fitted with the accepted culture of the time demands the salary of a prince and the services of a maid or two.

Too bad that those lads above the pig pen have to be taught someday the sad luxury of being proper.

I hope that I haven't given the impression that so far as raising a family is concerned the fundamental difference between village and city is that one has space and the other has not. A more important difference is that of attitude. Some of these newer urban developments do have space. They have taken to themselves far more good land than they had any moral right to, and some future and hungrier generation may one day curse the rest of us for letting them get away with it.

But even when a city has trees enough to go round there is still no assurance at all that a boy can simply sign up his pals as a construction crew and begin putting his imagination into a building of some sort. Urban living is essentially one of rules and regulations, at least so far as youngsters are concerned. There is apparently no limit to the number and variety of rules that adults can think up when they have nothing better to do than to get terribly serious about this business of child-rearing. I see by a recent issue of *Newsweek* that down in Riverhead, New York, the building inspector has suddenly got himself all excited over tree-houses. Says he's going to make them safe come hail or high water, and, with the straightest face in town, has drawn up these regulations:

> *No one is to build a tree-house without a duly authorized permit.*
> *No tree-house is allowed to be more than 12 feet off the ground. Walls must be at least 42 inches high and floor boards at least one inch thick. Houses must be framed by two-by-fours and attached, with 16 penny nails, to branches no less than five inches in diameter for hardwood trees and seven inches for softwood. . . .*

Aside from the fact that this fervent building inspector provides proof of how much some people want to worry about kids today, he also confesses a staggering ignorance of the one basic reason for a tree-house. Doesn't he know that it isn't supposed to be safe?

I think that this modern compulsion to take charge of our youngsters' leisure and play may be largely due to the fact that play has now become so serious to those of us who are old enough to know better. Surely one of the minor tragedies of our time is the fact that while we have more leisure than ever before, we seldom seem able to enjoy it in a leisurely fashion. One just doesn't play for the fun of it anymore. That's much too haphazard, and besides, it is simply not a mark of good breeding. If you want to play golf, you must do it correctly and with the proper professional instruction. You'll need a text book or two on the sport as well. If you want to go hiking, you don't just take off to the wilderness like the great speckled bird of the Old Testament — you join an Audubon society or some other kind of outdoor club with the proper prestige, so that you can take your hobby as seriously as possible, so you can meet other people who are equally serious about making sure that one's spare time isn't taken lightly.

And don't make the mistake of thinking that you can just pick up a bat and go barging into the young lad's ball game either. His play is now organized, supervised and pressurized by some Club, or by somebody who has special training and talent at firing so much team spirit into a youngster that he may not eat his breakfast for three days after the game, if his team should lose.

Now I'd like to ask some of these team spirit specialists what was so wrong with the old days, when a bunch of lads could just choose up sides and play a sport that might have been somewhat unscientific and amateurish, but was nevertheless so thoroughly enjoyable that you could talk about it and glow about it for years after.

Maybe that kind of play is just too inexpensive to have a place in today's affluent society. Or maybe we would put too many college-trained coaches out of work if we went back to it. But even if you get me to agree that our present craze for trained supervision for our children's sports is now necessary, I still want to know why it is so important for a boy to think it is a soul-searing disgrace to lose once in awhile. Can any sport be really enjoyed when a loss is so terrible?

I remember that when we used to be playing pasture-lot baseball at home, we knew exactly what to expect if we started to fight. Our Dad would come down the lane, pick up the ball and bat and take it back to the house with him.

"A game is for fun," he used to say, "and if the fun's over, the game ought to be over too."

Which to me still makes mighty good sense.

I have never made any scholarly study of the psychology of play but I am pretty certain that the intended purpose of the game is to encourage individuality. To encourage the player to outwit or outmanoeuvre a rival by doing something original and unexpected. If I am right in this, how can we justify today's expensively trained coach or playground supervisor who spends weeks mapping out strategy and key moves and then on the day of the game, directs every minute of play from the sidelines?

In the pasture-lot sports of my day none of the great people ever got in the way and we never worried about the lack of rule books. If we were suddenly in need of a new rule, we had no trouble inventing one. Sometimes indeed, we invented a whole new game. We had a game called "rag" for instance in which a team armed with sharpened broomsticks tried to carry a gunny sack through the other team's goal. A somewhat more dangerous variation of this unique sport was to substitute a pitch-fork for the broomstick and the hipbone of a cow for the gunnysack.

We were particularly original, I think, at devising ways to flavour a game with sex. One such pastime that I remember for reasons all my own was called "Partner Hide-And-Seek." The usual rules applied here with one important difference. Instead of playing as individuals, each hid with a chosen partner. It goes without saying that the partner was of the opposite sex and that the game was always played after dark. The particular game that I don't want to forget — the one that tried to make a man of me overnight — took place under a beautiful harvest moon in a field ranked with shadowy oat stocks. It never occurred to our parents apparently that the chief interest of this sport was more biological than anything else. They never seemed to worry even when the game stretched into midnight because some of the older couples just couldn't be found.

I suppose that parents never really believe that any youngster of theirs could do the same things they did when they were young.

There was another delightful little game which was for boys only and which could be played only at the old swimming hole. No one wore bathing suits in those days. Never thought of it. And the object of this sport was as uncomplicated as it was Spartan. First you hunted along the shallows next to the shore till you caught yourself a fair-sized crayfish. (To any city reader who has stayed with me this far I hasten to explain that this is the belligerent little crustacean which looks and acts exactly like a baby lobster.) Then when each had the crayfish of his choice he took his turn holding the angry little creature in front of his pecker until one of the claws took hold firmly enough to let him hang there. The boy who could suffer his crayfish the longest was the day's hero. A few seconds was generally enough.

Chapter Nine

❖❖❖❖❖❖❖❖❖❖❖❖❖❖❖❖❖❖❖❖❖❖❖❖❖

Back in our barefoot days every back door seemed to have its dog, but I can never recall anyone buying such an animal. You either got a pup from a neighbour, or you sneaked some flea-bitten outcast into the household when your parents were too distressed with more important worries to notice you. And many a girl's first tremulous deception was when she smuggled some blue-tongued, half-starved kitten into her room by hiding it under her shimmy. But even after the tearful battles with your mother were over, it was a conditional peace which followed. It was always clearly understood then that both pet and youngster were on their best behaviour and that the feeding and the comfort of the animal was the full responsibility of the boy or girl who had been guilty of bringing the little beast into the family.

Backward! Turn backward oh Time in your flight! Pets are both an industry and a fashion now and the itchy old cur who used to sleep behind the woodbox has been replaced by a creature with a pedigree which is much more illustrious than that of the owner. He's far too costly for a younster to buy himself and often too valuable to entrust to the care of any amateur.

Our dog was a half-grown collie which just wandered in one cold day to ask for a handout. "Now let's not start coddling a dog like that!" our father warned us as he flipped the humble animal over and checked its plumbing. "It's another female."

But when the snow began to whip off the tops of the drifts that night and the collie had found a way to look through the kitchen window to watch us eat supper, it was Dad himself who brought her inside and fed her. "First time in my life I ever saw a dog with a blue belly," he said as she rolled over on her back to say thank you.

And since I was the one who had first pleaded her case and it was my pants she slept on at night, she became my dog. It was up to me to housebreak her and mop up her mistakes. And I was the one who claimed the right to name her. Seems to me now that I had a rather literary name all picked out for her but whatever it was doesn't matter now. "Ah! just call her 'Squat'!" father said one evening when he saw me going for the mop again. And Squat she was from that day on.

I saw that she got her share of the table scraps. I patched up the gash a groundhog put on her leg. It was I who got pliers and relieved her of the quills from her first porcupine. And when the summer brought so much itch that she spent half of her time scratching, I rubbed her with some of the sulphur and lard that my Uncle Bill mixed up for me. "Fixes me up all right," he told me. "Why wouldn't it work for a dog? You just have to put a bit more sulphur with it, that's all, else she'll eat it off." Uncle Bill had a cure for worms too. "You just make yourself some spaghetti with all the garlic in it that you can stand to eat and you give her the bottom of the pot to clean out and she'll get cleaned out too. Just try it."

And Bill also had a cheap and ready cure when Squat got somewhat snow-blinded from chasing too many jackrabbits into the setting sun. He took an especially thoughtful chaw of Big Ben eating tobacco, looked Squat square in the face, told her that it would only hurt for a second and then spat a squirt in each eye.

Squat saw things much more clearly in a week or so.

Keeping the nation's dogs free of such things as mange, worms and bloodshot eyes is a very serious profession now, and a very expensive one. It takes thousands of men in white and hundreds of clinics to keep a mutt full of beans today. In the city of Toronto we have a dog psychologist. Does your pooch have a split personality or an inferiority complex? Quick! Get him to Toronto!

Is it any wonder that the faithful, tail-happy cur which God, in one of His better moments, put on earth to teach His favourite humans the full meaning of love is now so often a crochety aristocrat and good for nothing but a prestige symbol? Please, you city people who are on your way out to share the country with us, won't you get over the idea that your dog is too valuable for a rowdy youngster to play with? And so beautiful he must be protected from mud, burrs, groundhogs, heifer-dust and everything else that is natural?

I am appalled that even such an indestructible child's toy as a Shetland pony has now become so precious and fashionable a commodity that only expert horsemen and show people should be entrusted with his care and training. At our fair just last week one of the magnificently equipped exhibitors from New York State came to me after my own young lad had just earned a red ribbon in one of the pony classes.

"That's a very, very fine animal you have there," he told me. "But he should have a real handler to bring out the best in him. Not that I've got anything against that boy of yours. He's a mighty fine boy. But there's just nothing that will spoil a pony so quick you know, as to give him over to a kid. . . ."

He looked like a very intelligent man, even if he was from New York. I wonder what in hell he thinks a pony is for anyhow? To strut and prance in the approved fashion in a show ring? To entertain comfortable old men who have too much money and time on their hands?

I would guess that of all the urgings which tempt urban parents to move into the country, none is quite so hard to shrug aside as those of the children bouncing ecstatically at the very thought of it. "And we could have a pony out there too, couldn't we Daddy? . . . . Well not right away maybe but someday, someday when we get a few debts paid . . . . Couldn't we Daddy? Couldn't we . . . ?"

For the pony is something more than one of the most glamorous animals dear to childhood. He is one of those pets which even the most spoiled of children cannot dream of owning so long as Mamma and Daddy live in the city. One may own any kind of dog or cat in the city so long as one promises to keep said pet harmless, sexless, and odourless. But a pony is one of the interesting animals which cannot comply with the propriety of urban life. Even the smallest one is too big.

And the goat is another animal which every child has a right to meet and cannot until he is turned loose in country meadows. The reason here is a little different from that which puts the hex on a pony, however. The deodorant people seem to have convinced us all now that chlorophyll is the magic ingredient which will allow anti-social humans to get closer to one another, but the billy goat lives on chlorophyll and it doesn't seem to do a thing for him. To anyone but a boy, he stinks!

But there is another kind of pet possible only in the country which some of us find more rewarding than even the most lovable of the familiar pets. I am referring to those birds and animals which cost nothing but a young lad's unforgettable adventure in bringing them home from the woods. I am sure that there is an appeal in these pets borrowed from the wild that springs from something far deeper than their novelty. Perhaps it does something for a man's education to make the acquaintance of animals we can never hope to master completely — animals who consider themselves lords of creation the same as we do. It is significant, I think, that so many of the great animal stories of the last decade concern pets which have never been caged or conquered. Gavin Maxwell's otters in his *Ring of Bright Water* come and go as freely as a pair of bachelors. And in Rowena Farr's *Seal Morning* the cottage door is always open so that her seal may leave whenever the sea beyond should call.

The list of recent titles devoted to off-trail pets could easily fill a page. There are the three books by Joy Adams about her lions; Peter Krott's beautiful story about his wolverines — the supposedly untameable devils from the Arctic; John Patrick Gillese's *Kirby's Gander,* Eric Lambert's *Dolphin,* and Sterling North's coon story, *Rascal* — and these are only a few of the books of this nature which one could mention.

At our own home we had a weakness for pet crows. Every spring some of us boys would go through the woods trying to spot a nest we could reach, and once this was located one of us would make the hazardous climb for the initial inspection. Such a climb was hazardous for two reasons. Crows have a habit of building high up and in trees which are very difficult to scale. Secondly, once an intruder had finally kneed his way to the nest the parent crows would swoop down on him with terrifying courage and ferocity, especially if the young were already hatched. One trip was rarely enough for, as every country boy knew, you could not take a crow from the nest and expect to raise him unless he was fully feathered and almost ready to fly. If you kidnapped him while he was still naked and all belly and mouth, he would likely die a shivering death a few days later. So generally you watched your nest carefully, climbing up again and again, until the noisy occupants had outgrown their last pinfeathers and seemed even bigger and better feathered than the older ones who were threatening to peck your eyes out if you didn't leave them alone. Finally, you selected the best one in the nest, put it inside your shirt and started the perilous descent back to earth.

No one who has never fed a pet crow into independence will ever believe how much such a bird can eat, and the only consolation his guardian has in the matter is that when he is hungry a young crow will eat almost anything. So you start your project trying to dig enough juicy earthworms to fill the ravenous maw, but in a few days that will have become such an impossible task that you will resort to bread and milk or oatmeal, or just about anything that is left over from the table. And somehow or other the marvellous digestive system of the crow allows him to survive. Certainly the frightful persistence of his cawing rarely allows a human to starve him to death.

By the time your crow is two weeks old he is following you all over the yard, hollering for something more at your every step. By the time he has begun to fly he is likely to find you where you are at work in the fields and light on your shoulder to voice his complaints. I recall one crow which spent most of the day with us at our hoeing, and after he had been batted off first one shoulder and then another, he selected one of the fat-backed mares in the nearby pasture and rode bare-back all day to voice his disappointment in us. When your young pet has lost the last of his youthful awkwardness and his feathers are so shining with black that the sun puts a green glint in them, he will begin to find his own food.

At our place I think the only reason our practical father tolerated crows at all was because they could be counted on to pick the bugs from the potato plants — a rare good turn indeed before the coming of our modern insecticides. But a pet crow never seemed to desert us even after he had found ways and means to find his own victuals, and that attachment could be counted on to persist until his wild cousins from the swamps beyond began to congregate and summon the clan for the flight south. There would be a rather dramatic day or two in Indian Summer when our crow would fly farther and farther away from home base; when our crow and the others would finally get acquainted, distantly calling at first, then sitting on adjacent fence posts to argue social status, then finally flying off, with our crow almost lost in the flock but still quarreling. He might leave the flock once or twice, but inevitably came that incredibly quiet November morning when he was no longer swearing at us when we opened the back door to the morning; when there were no caustic remarks aimed at us from the clothes-line as we made our pilgrimages to the backhouse.

And breakfast was strangely sober that morning with some little sisters crying perhaps and all of us feeling secretly guilty about not treating our pet more kindly when we had him. After all, it was ourselves that made him an orphan, wasn't it? *"Do you suppose it was because we didn't feed him anymore and didn't love him enough anymore that made him leave us, Mama?"*

For even in the most kindly of families, there was something about a crow's personality which made it very difficult to forgive him his trespasses. He had the eye of an eagle, the imagination of a restless little girl and the evil genius of Peck's bad boy. And when I think of the genius for evil in crows I am thinking in particular of a crow named Jim which belonged to one of my younger brothers. I see by a recent issue of the hometown paper in one of those quaint inside columns entitled "Forty Years Ago" that on one occasion Jim flew right across the village to follow my brother to school one September morning. We had a little farm on the edge of the village then and the old school was clear across town more than a mile away. I am not sure just what guidance Jim may have received from co-operative school boys that morning but the fact is that he did find his way through a window which opened into the upper classroom where my brother sat and came marching sedately over to his desk, much to the delight of everyone but the master.

But even feats as endearing as this one way didn't save Jim from many a scutching. There were times indeed when he came within an ace of being executed. Had one of our brothers or sisters been so incurably inquisitive I suppose that we would have expected him to become an Edison or an Einstein, but Jim's inquisitiveness didn't give us the same feeling of awe at all. The whole human race seemed to be a major study for Jim and on those days when no amount of cawing could induce anyone to give him a handout, he would sometimes become strangely quiet as he gave himself to a study of some aspect of civilized life. He would sit on a line of freshly hung clothes, for instance, testing a clothes-pin first. And if it wouldn't come loose, he would become deeply absorbed in the colour, texture, and possible uses of the various items of clothing flapping in the sun. A pair of newly polished shoes set out on the back stoop might end up half way across the barnyard if they didn't weigh too much, and the laces might never be found. And woe betide the bright toy or trinket which a youngster might carelessly leave on the porch. The fascination which bright things had for Jim made something of a pervert of him.

The morning our mother threatened to have Jim duly executed was a Sunday when she made the mistake of dropping her brooch on the pump stand while she rescued the baby from the mud just beyond. She set it down for only an instant, but that instant was long enough for Jim to retrieve the glittering object and fly off with it.

Now that in itself would have been terrible enough because that brooch was practically the only thing resembling jewelry which Mother owned. But there was another side to Jim's perversion which is almost too delicate to mention here. Among those aspects of human life which he found most intriguing was the backhouse, and many a morning he sought his privacy, sunning himself out of the wind, looking from time to time into the mysterious depths, first with one eye and then the other, and muttering drily to himself as if to say "And this is the creature who's supposed to be only a little lower than the angels!"

Now there were two very serious objections to Jim's claiming the backhouse as his study. First of all on those days when he contemplated longest and hardest there, he cast aspersions of a non-vocal nature which rarely, if ever, went down through the holes built for that purpose and into the mysterious depths below. Secondly, the backhouse was the place where Jim loved to enjoy the trinkets and other bright objects for which he had an insatiable addiction. And then, after turning the object over and over in his witch's claws and testing it with his beak until it held no further novelty for him, he would simply drop it down through one of the breezy openings behind him.

Which is undoubtedly what Mother had in mind when the broom went sailing through the air that Sunday morning with enough accuracy to make Jim drop her brooch before he was half-way to his goal. "Henry!" she cried to Dad when she picked her precious ornament out of the long grass and brushed it off, "Henry! I want you to get rid of that crow and the sooner the better! I mean it, Henry!"

Mother was rarely capable of violence and some of the younger ones were on the verge of tears because they were so sure that Jim had been irrevocably condemned to death. Like all righteous executions however Jim's fated hour was postponed and postponed again until we had begun to hope that the whole trouble was safely forgotten. And then suddenly Jim redeemed himself completely and in the most unexpected way imaginable.

It happened on a Saturday afternoon that the smokingest of our uncles came to visit us and trade roosters. Now Uncle Bill, like all of the rest of our uncles and every other non-Christian around, knew full well that in our house there was no smoking allowed. Absolutely. You snuffed out your pipe and put it in your pocket before you stuck your head through the door. Only Uncle Bill, in deference to Mother's holy hate of tobacco, did things a little differently that afternoon. There was a little tool shelf just outside the summer kitchen door, and before he went in for the traditional cup of tea and apple pie, he not only put his dead pipe there but his plug of smoking tobacco as well. A smoking plug was a rather lovely thing in those days, golden yellow, manfully aromatic, and with no need of either package or advertisement. But each plug did carry one small decoration — a glistening little tin heart stapled to its middle and bearing the name of the brand.

Uncle Bill was one of the more leisurely members of my father's bustling family, and by the time he had finished his second cup of tea and his third piece of apple pie, Jim had finished his detailed study of the smoking plug he had pilfered from the tool shelf and taken to the backhouse. And by the time Uncle Bill discovered what had happened and began to explode at him, Jim had dropped the plug where Mother had always thought all tobacco should go.

Mother and Jim seemed to get along somewhat better after that.

Chapter Ten

❖❖❖❖❖❖❖❖❖❖❖❖❖❖❖❖❖❖❖❖❖❖❖❖

Statisticians tell us that our sons and daughters are not likely to marry at so tender an age as we did, and some of the God-people will be quick to ascribe this change to the coming of the pill and the new morality. It seems to me however that the reason is clearly economic. Before today's young couple can commit matrimony they must buy an array of household equipment and appliances which, even when kept to the very minimum and procured with the lowest down-payment possible, is likely to starve their love for years. It seems hard to believe now that within living memory there was a time when about all one had to do to begin the weary endurance of married bliss was to find the right partner. Beyond that, the furnishings required were so few and so cheap that it is a wonder the free enterprise system was able to survive. There were in fact but three principal parts to yesterday's village household — a kitchen stove, a bed and a parlour. Everything else was incidental and easily obtained. Pots, pans, dishes, lamps, chairs and quilts could be bought for a song at the first auction, if indeed they couldn't be scrounged from the home to which the bridal couple belonged.

And the loveliest aspect of this forgotten simplicity was that no one was impatient with it. Even when the marvel of electricity began to cautiously reach out from Main Street and Crown Hill into the back streets, I can never recall us thinking that we were particularly backward because we still did our homework by the smoky glow of coal oil lamps.

"Oh it would be nice to have one of them little electric motors and give Mom running water for her kitchen," I remember Father saying. "But then we already have running water, don't we Mom? Whenever you need water I run and fetch it!"

Electricity did finally come to our home, though not until I came home again after the war, and home was never quite the same again. It would be wrong to say that its cosiness was gone however, for the same stove was still in the kitchen, still the centre of everything. And to this day I have never quite forgiven fashion for decreeing the ousting of the old-fashioned kitchen range. These modern affairs are no doubt one of the more striking manifestations of modern science and artistic design, and I would not argue for a moment that they haven't made the preparation of a good meal a more pleasant chore now than it was in Mother's day. Nor would I cast any reflection on their cleanliness. Why shouldn't they be clean? They have no tricky damper, no hungry firebox, no messy ash-pit. The kitchen stove of today has neither breath nor any other suggestion of bodily function. It is as gleamingly immaculate and sterile as a piece of hospital equipment, whatever life it has being sustained by automatically controlled intravenous injections of oil, gas or electricity.

And the soul has gone out of it too. Nobody pays much attention to it anymore. It is no longer the hub of the house.

Now, the old cast-iron range was something more than a device for putting the pots to boil. It was ideally suited for doing an infinite variety of household tasks, while at the same time providing a quietly delightful focal point for whatever leisure might be left to a family on a wintry night.

There was the warming closet, for instance, which was about as versatile a kitchen appliance as anything which has ever been manufactured. It could, at one and the same time, shelter several loaves of rising dough, keep a tardy man's supper warm, dry the wet snowy mittens and stocking caps of at least six youngsters, and stow a brace of flat-irons and several pounds of smaller items which never seemed to have any better place to go.

Then there was the admirable invention known as the reservoir. The best of them were lined with copper and there was even one deluxe model once which boasted a spigot at the bottom. The reservoir, in case you are too long away from such things to remember, was attached to the far end of the oven and held the water which you carefully caught and matured in the rain barrel.

There were other features too, which, for sheer ingenuity and convenience, no modern stove has ever yet equalled. There was the shuttered draft at the top of the firebox through which a smoking man could insert a sliver of cedar and light his pipe a dozen times per hour without the expenditure of a single match. Then there was the alcove beneath, which was exactly right for the dog, and the torrid space above the woodbox at the back which was perfect for hiding a line of drying diapers.

But best of all was the comfort of the oldtime oven. I remember, that on the great day when the family was selecting the stove which became ours, the one thing my father seemed most concerned with was the strength of the oven door. "Can you stand on it when it's open?" my father asked the merchant. And when the merchant invited my father to step up onto the door with him, the sale was made.

For the first function of an oven door in those days was not to close up the oven at all. It was primarily a place for a tired man to rest his weary chilblains while he read, or talked to his wife, or helped the kids with their homework. And I'll defy anyone to show me a more pleasant place to spend a winter's evening than in a chair beside an oven full of drying birch or poplar. The kind of chair doesn't really matter, just so long as a man can tilt it back on its hind legs enough to get his feet onto the rim of that oven door.

Which is why there is still an oldtime, tile-backed, wood-smoking range on this farm of mine — one which holds a circle of warm friends in spite of the blare of colour television in the next room. And if a couple of the critics should actually read a chapter or two of this book before composing their scholarly reviews of it, and if they should find its prose too lazy to be literary, maybe that old stove should take part of the blame. Because much of this has been written with my sock feet on its oven door.

Chapter Eleven

✤✤✤✤✤✤✤✤✤✤✤✤✤✤✤✤✤✤✤✤✤✤✤✤✤✤

An information bulletin circulated to arouse the public's interest in the great Canadian baking industry has just drawn my attention to the fact that ninety-five out of every hundred housewives today buy bread from the baker; and the bulletin contrasts this figure with some pride to the fact that just fifty years ago only eight of that hundred asked the baker for the staff of life.

I must confess that I cannot interpret such a change as progress. I am merely led to a sad state of wonderment as to why, if Mother's bread had to go by the way of the horse and buggy and breast-fed babies, the bakers couldn't have given us something as good.

Nor will it do to tell me that it is only the memories of childhood which have attached themselves to this product and made of it the perfect thing that I claim it to be. That there were memories connected with the making of the bread back home, I would be the last to deny for this was an institution which was almost as fascinating as it was important. First there was the buying of the yeast, which meant a trip down the road for one of us to the grocery with three cents sweating comfortably in the grip of the hand. Then the trip to the cellar for the carefully hoarded potato water, the cranking of the old sifter which was always out of round, and then the waiting for the dough to rise. But most of all I remember that portion of the ceremony where the dough was to be punched. It was a job admirably suited to the energetic fists of children, but the only trouble was that if a boy did not take enough time to first wash his hands as thoroughly as Mama had warned him to, the evidence would come off as soon as he tangled up with his work, and the dough in the immediate vicinity of the unscoured fist would take on a tattle-tale gray that no amount of punching could quite sink out of sight.

71

And finally the great pans went into the oven. The oven of our old Happy Thought range had a crack which let in the light and smoke, and sometimes when we forgot to turn the loaves in time, one side would be as black as the oven itself.

But when the batch was right a loaf would come out looking for all the world like a big, plump, Buff Orpington hen, with the great thick ledges drooping from the rim marks as if her wings were let down to cluck.

It is the taste however which I will always remember longest and one cannot describe taste with words, even the words of a poet. Why, oh why, haven't our bakers been able to at least recapture some element of that taste for us? That they unwittingly admit the superiority of that old home-cooked loaf is evident from the fact that there has never been a bakery anywhere which hasn't at some time or other concocted a product which, with more hope than honesty, they have labelled "Homemade," or something like that. But why haven't these efforts ever tasted homemade? Why must the loaf which comes from the baker's basket always smell and taste as if it had been baked under such frightfully sterile conditions that all flavour and aroma have evaporated along with the antiseptic or deodorant or whatever it was that kicked out the germs and plugged the loaf so marvellously full of balance and vitamins?

Could it be the spray gun which puts that lovely old oak lacquer on the crust? Could it be the yeast they use? Are they absolutely certain that the brewers haven't used that yeast first before passing it on to them? Or is it simply that the modern baker has never devised a way of approximating such mysterious factors as those contributed by a cracked oven, or by motherly pride, or by a boy's grimy fists in the dough?

Chapter Twelve

❖❖❖❖❖❖❖❖❖❖❖❖❖❖❖❖❖❖❖❖❖❖❖❖

With another record cost-of-living index posted, it seems to me that harrassed housewives across this country must be thinking back now to the days when their mothers, on allowances of $10 a week or less, were somehow able to feed the family well enough to keep everyone healthy.

I remember the favorite reply my father had when some of the neighbours would meet him downtown and ask him how everyone was at home. "All able to eat!" he would say.

Well, how were we able to eat back in those days? And how were we able to get our vitamins along with that eating in a time when most grocers didn't even stock such items as tomato juice and California lettuce in the winter, and when even oranges were often for Christmas only?

The fact is that there *were* other sources of vitamins to supplement the flour bin and the pork barrel. We had apples till mid-winter at least, and sometimes, Lord willing, there was enough money for us to have prunes or raisins or apricots. One of the reasons we got those items relatively cheaply was because we didn't have to pay for any technicoloured packaging or television commercials then. These dried fruits came north in 20-pound wooden boxes — boxes you could afterward make into medicine cabinets or bedroom bookshelves.

But it seems to me as I look back on those impossible days that a great deal of credit for balancing out our diet belonged to the humble, homely-smelling old kraut barrel. Do you remember it now? How, when the first flints of snow began to pelt the dead leaves, your mother and father would bring out the wooden cabbage-cutter. Looked something like a giant carpenter's plane turned upside down. And then after we kids had washed each head thoroughly and checked the outer leaves for any bowel movements the worms might have cast on them, the cabbages were shredded one by one by sliding them over the knife in the middle of the board. The accumulation of shreds were then packed into the waiting barrel with a careless hand full of salt here and there. It was important to pack the kraut down tight, and while I'm sure our modern health worriers will blanch at the thought, that packaging was often accomplished by the simple expedient of placing a vigorous youngster of the right size into the barrel to stomp it down with his bare feet. Well, what's so wrong with that? His feet were washed — generally.

Finally, when the barrel was tramped full and tight, a loose lid was put on the top and weighted down with a big stone, and the barrel was manoeuvred into some dark corner of the cellar, there to brew like silage without any further human help.

A few weeks later, after many a supposedly secret sampling, the kraut was declared ready; and as long as I live I will never forget how indescribably delicious that kraut would smell when you came in on a winter's evening, hungry from hockey on the pond or a day in the woods, and your mother would have it in the frying pan sizzling along with the fried potatoes and onions and salt pork. Best thing in the world to prevent rheumatism, my dad used to say, and he's eighty-six now and still has no rheumatism.

Brought some sauerkraut home the other night, not for my rheumatism but mainly for sentimental reasons. Bought it at the delicatessen's in a quart jar for 55 cents and slipped it into a frying pan for supper when no one was looking. And do you know what my kids said when they came in after basketball practice a few minutes later?

"Oh! What is that frightful smell? Oh, Daddy! No! Please, please throw it out before you make us all sick!"

You know there are times like that when I feel very old.

Chapter Thirteen

✦✦✦✦✦✦✦✦✦✦✦✦✦✦✦✦✦✦✦✦✦✦✦

This young lad of mine who owns the tree house in the yard came to me with a rather surprising request last week.

"Dad," he said, "could you buy me a mattress? One of those rubber kinds you blow up? It doesn't feel so hot sleeping on a floor as hard as that one."

My billfold was flatter than usual just then so I made some small protest. "I thought the wind in the tree would rock you to sleep before you could notice the boards," I said.

"Just rocks you onto the bolts," I was told. (The floor was once the tail gate of an old truck.)

"Well, then," I said, "what would be wrong with a straw tick?"

He didn't get the idea at all. "Straw tick?" he repeated. "Sounds like some sort of insect!"

And while I was trying to explain the meaning of the term, and to suggest that he could very well make one himself by lacing two big bran sacks together, I began to wonder how many adults can still recall those rustic days when a straw tick was what one expected to find in all but the most pretentious of country bedrooms. And in case you aren't one of those with so long a memory, I should explain right now that by "straw tick" I mean the old-fashioned mattress which was once made by filling a big canvas envelope with fresh straw. Or do you remember it now?

Remember how the ragweed stems and the thistles were always poking through at you? Remember the way the straw would rustle all night in your ear as if it were full of mice? Remember the time it *was* full of mice?

Well, no matter what your memories might be, you will agree that a straw-filled tick wasn't a very comfortable affair. The worst thing I can recall was the valley of depression which always developed right down the middle of it. If you slept two in a bed, you were forever rolling into each other's arms whether you wanted to or not. Not a bad idea for a married couple given to spats perhaps, but for feuding youngsters it never solved a thing.

And if you slept three in a bed, as we often did in those days, one of the three simply dropped down into the valley and the other two just rolled over top of him. Kept him mighty warm, too, if he knew how to keep from smothering.

In our house, however, not all of the mattresses were made of straw. There was one good store-bought spring mattress under our humble roof, but that was a very special property which belonged to Mother and Dad. Nor did it ever occur to any of the rest of us to resent that discrimination at all. Comfort, in our way of life then, was never a birthright. It was a rare luxury which came as a fitting reward for years of long toil and of doing without. And though we children worked a lot harder than today's glittering crowd of youth would ever dream possible, we still didn't feel that we were entitled to any particular thanks. On the contrary, and in spite of the bitter protests we sometimes made, we felt indebted to our parents.

Not that I'd like to institute a system of straw ticks in my own home, but I wonder sometimes, and rather bitterly, if there isn't some way I can convince my demanding offspring that the world does not owe them a living merely because they had the good fortune to be born. And that comfort and luxury are things that can never really be appreciated until you earn them.

But then I also got to thinking that getting bitter is a sign of getting old, so I went downtown and got the young lad the mattress he wanted.

Chapter Fourteen

❖❖❖❖❖❖❖❖❖❖❖❖❖❖❖❖❖❖❖❖❖❖❖❖

W hen I saw a Model-T Ford kicking up its venerable heels on a back country road the other day I felt that rather shocked pleasure experienced by one who suddenly comes face to face with a friend he has long believed dead. Which was somewhat foolish, of course, because no one who has ever shared any part of his younger days with a Model-T should be surprised at finding such an astoundingly durable creature living to a ripe old age.

It was a remarkable machine that Model-T, but I think that what makes us remember it so warmly now was the fact that it gave so many evidences of being something other than a machine. It was a personage. It had character. It had a name, Lizzie, and as that name implies, it had a sex as well. Moreover, it possessed all the exasperating and unpredictable moods of that sex. Yet somehow I never think of the Model-T Lizzie as being so closely akin to the human who struggled with her as she was to the horse.

Such an idea may have sprung, I suppose, from the fact that Lizzie evolved from the horse, yet there were points of similarity between the two which were more than imagination. There was that little ritual of starting her, for instance. When you went around to her head to ready her for the day's task, you could seldom escape that same sense of nervous doubt that you would feel in approaching a high-spirited and fickle filly. You murmured reassurances, patted her gently on the hood, and wound the crank two or three times in a clockwise direction. But for all your profession of faith and goodwill, you were never sure what would happen and you cautiously draped your thumb on the outside of the handle so that if by chance Lizzie still held any

78

grudge from your last encounter with her, the kick of a backfire
wouldn't break your wrist.

On the other hand, the most casual coaxing would often see
her so "raring to go" that she could hardly wait for you to climb
on her back, and she would ease her quivering haunches toward
you like an eager mare chomping at the bit to be off on her
morning canter.

But she could be as aggravating as the worst horse on the
farm. Sometimes she would only partially balk. She would re-
fuse to take a certain hill perhaps, until you turned her end for
end, so that she couldn't see the job ahead of her, and then she
would quite willingly take the hill backwards. Sometimes the
balk would be complete, but the mere lifting of the hood or a
loving tap on the coil box would sweeten her will. Other times
all the power and persuasion of Hades itself couldn't persuade
her to snort a syllable. I recall one such time, however, when
after cranking, cajoling, pulling, pushing and tinkering until I
was blue in the gills, I simply kicked her in the nose. The effect
was magical. She started up as if the wits had been scared out of
her and I had no more trouble with her all that day. The radiator
had one more wrinkle in its furrowed brow though, and that was
a problem of a different kind.

Eventually everybody's Lizzie had radiator trouble but in the
country at least, this was never thought serious. There were several standard cures for leaks and none of them costly. You could
simply drop the raw whites of a couple of eggs into the radiator
and then let your motor run hard enough and long enough to
bring the water to a boil. When you saw the lines of hard-boiled
egg white peeking out where the leaks used to be you knew you
had done a good job. A few teaspoons of dry mustard or a hand-
ful of finely ground pig feed was also supposed to plug a leaky
radiator, and the fact that it must have plugged off a lot of the
circulation as well never seemed to worry anyone, Lizzie included. If you happened to be on the road when the radiator sprang
a leak you went scouting for a horse bun, preferably fresh, and
dropped this into the system before filling the radiator up again
from the ditch.

There was a time of course, before the cantankerous traits of
old age had settled on Lizzie — the time when she first came to

our yard in all the prim black splendour of an old maid out visiting on a spring Sunday. Our hens had as yet not roosted above her, there wasn't a boot on any one of her tires — not even on the spare — and hanging about her was a delightful aroma that was somewhere between that of new harness and the fabrikoid bindings on our *Books of Knowledge*. We boys would have been highly privileged that day had we been allowed so much as to screw down the radiator cap. But what I remember most sharply of that morning was how we lay on our backs in her cool, oily shade, looking up at her unblemished front for no other reason than to quietly marvel at how huge and powerful she seemed!

Chapter Fifteen

❖❖❖❖❖❖❖❖❖❖❖❖❖❖❖❖❖❖❖❖❖❖❖❖❖

T here were six boys in our family and only two girls, but our overworked mother never complained about such an unfortunate ratio. She simply and firmly insisted that each of her boys do his share of the housework. So it was that we churned, scrubbed floors, washed dishes, peeled potatoes, made beds, spun the washing machine, changed the baby's diapers and took our turn doing just about all of the chores generally regarded as feminine. And the results were sometimes unexpectedly dramatic. I recall for instance a certain summer's day when our baby brother of that year was committed to the care of another brother who must have been ten or eleven at the time. His assignment was not particularly strenuous but still exacting enough to keep him out of our father's workshop, where he dearly loved to tinker. He was to keep his little brother clean, dry and safe — "safe" meaning that the baby was to be kept from toddling into danger and from trying to eat such things as mud and worms.

Sometime during the morning, her suspicions probably aroused by a curious lack of complaint, our mother went to the kitchen door to see how well her commands were being carried out and let out a shriek that shook the windows. For there, sitting with the dog in the yard and blissfully unaware of the horror of it all, was the baby with what appeared to be a long black snake wriggling up his leg.

A closer look however revealed that the wriggling snake was a small rubber tube which ran all the way up the inside of one fat little leg where it disappeared under the diaper. And when Mother indignantly yanked off the diaper to trace the mystery to its source she uncovered a most remarkable piece of engineering. For the upper end of the tube fitted over the spout of a small funnel which had been securely taped over the baby's spout.

81

The brother responsible for this invention was meanwhile quite oblivious to all the commotion he had caused. He was over in the beloved workshop, whistling softly over his next project and when Mother hauled him out by an ear to explain himself, he was quite insulted. "I was just sick and tired of changing wet diddies!" he whimpered.

The diaper, it must be admitted, was still quite dry.

For everyone but mother the affair of the funnel was good for many a laugh all that summer. And the fact that forty years later we can laugh as hard as ever about it is proof of how disgustingly primitive country humour can be. For reasons I gladly leave to the psychologists to unravel, our jokes were rarely subtle in those days, and they had a tendency to involve the baser bodily functions. Indeed as I look back at that time now it seems that our humour was seldom very far from the backhouse. Just as yesterday's kitchen seemed to be the hub of the family's industry and the cellar the centre of its thrift and the parlour the shrine of its meditation, so the lowly backhouse was the country seat of its wit. It was in fact practically impossible for the backhouse to enter into the conversation at all without inviting a special sort of smile. If one was assigned the task of putting a new window in the venerable old building or of lining it with new wallpaper, the worst part of the job was not the heavy air that you had to work in, but having to endure the smart-aleck comments of uncouth brothers and sisters who rejoiced in your degradation. A frost that killed our tomato plants was a sad misfortune but a frost which lined the backhouse portholes with icy whiskers' was merely playing a hilarious prank. A storm which tore the roof from the chicken house could move Mother to tears, but if instead the wind lifted the lid from the backhouse you could hardly wait to share the joke with the neighbours. And because the very thought of this unique establishment had a tendency to tickle the funny bone, we knew it by an endless variety of other names. We called it the Parliament Building, or Aunty's, or Seaterville, the Sit and Think, the Police Station, the Business Place, the Throne, the Grunt and Groan . . . . The backhouse actually had its own feast day too, because most of us young pagans were quite unaware of the fact that Hallowe'en was the night when the souls of the recently departed are getting their release from Purgatory. To us, it was the one night of the year when youth joined ranks in the dark to prove our contempt of age and authority by tipping every unfortified backhouse in the village. But more on this later, since our Hallowe'en revels deserve a chapter to themselves.

I have never known a critic who seemed to have taken any note of the fact, but a rather prolific bouquet of literature grew up around the country backhouse along with the hollyhocks and wild cucumbers. Tucked away in your grandfather's treasury of books you may still find a tattered copy of Chic Sale's *The Specialist,* which is the combined autobiography and trade secrets of the most famous backhouse builder of his day. And at some time or other, tacked up in practically every privy in the land (till Mother tore it down) was this poem. So far as I know, no author ever let his name be attached to this disgraceful bit of folk verse, but I have often suspected James Whitcomb Riley of being the guilty party.

ODE TO OUTDOOR PLUMBING

When memory keeps me company,
and moves to smiles or tears,
A weather-beaten object looms
through the mist of years:
Behind the house and barn it stood,
a half a mile or more,
The hurrying feet a path had made,
straight to the swinging door.
The architecture was a type of
simple classic art,
And in the tragedy of life, it
played a leading part;
And oft the passing reveller drove
slow and heaved a sigh,
To see the modest hired girl slip
out with glances shy.

We had our posey garden, that the
    women loved so well.
That filled the evening breezes so
    full of homey cheer,
And told the night-o'ertaken tramp
    that human life was near.
On lazy August afternoons it made
    a little bower
For there the summer morning its
    very cares entwined,
And berry bushes reddened in the
    steaming soil behind.

All day long fat spiders spun their
    webs to catch the buzzing flies,
That flitted to and from the house,
    where Ma was baking pies.
And once a swarm of hornets bold
    had built their palace there,
And stung my unsuspecting aunt
    — I must not tell you where;
Then father took a flaming pole
    — that was a happy day —
He nearly burned the building, but
    the hornets left to stay.
When summer bloom began to fade,
    and winter to carouse,
We banked the little building with
    a heap of hemlock boughs.

But when the crust was on the snow,
    and the sullen skies were gray,
In sooth the building was no place
    where one could wish to stay.
We did our duties promptly; there
    one purpose swayed in mind;
We tarried not, nor lingered long
    on what we left behind
The torture of that icy seat could
    make a Spartan sob,

For the needs must scrape the
   gooseflesh with a lacerating cob
That from a frost-encrusted nail
   was suspended by a string —
My father was a frugal man and
   wasted not a thing.

When grandpa had to "go out back"
   and make his morning call,
We'd bundle up the dear old man
   with a muffler and a shawl.
I knew the hole on which he sat,
   'twas padded all around
And once I dared to sit there,
   'twas all too wide, I found.
My loins were all too little, and I
   jack-knifed there to stay;
They had to come and get me out,
   or I'd have passed away.
Then father said ambition was a
   thing small boys should shun,
And I must use the children's hole
   till childhood days were done.

But still I marvel at the craft that
   cut the holes so true;
The baby hole, and the slender
   hole that fitted Sister Sue.
That dear old country landmark!
   I've travelled around a bit,
And in the lap of luxury has been
   my lot to sit;
But ere I die I'll eat the fruit of
   the trees I robbed of yore,
Then seek the shanty where my
   name is carved upon the door.
I ween the old familiar smell will
   soothe my faded soul:
I'm now a man, but nonetheless,
   I'll try the children's hole.

Chapter Sixteen

❖❖❖❖❖❖❖❖❖❖❖❖❖❖❖❖❖❖❖❖❖❖❖❖❖

To a lad with my Fundamentalist upbringing there were only four kinds of people so far as religion was concerned. There were first of all, people like my brawling, swearing uncles who made no pretence of any sort. There was probably some hope for them because they knew that they were living in sin and should there ever come a time when sin should lose its unusually powerful attraction for them, they might yet come to the light and be saved.

Then there were those comfortably hypocritical citizens who belonged to one of the fashionable Protestant churches in town — the Presbyterians, Anglicans and Methodists. There were some differences between these three, but if I interpreted my parents rightly, they wouldn't amount to a hill of beans on the Day of Judgment. The Presbyterians voted Liberal and were ridiculously conservative in their religion. The Anglicans voted Conservative and their religion was so shamelessly liberal they couldn't tell right from wrong. Come the Sabbath, a Presbyterian would hardly chase a fly from his porridge, while an Anglican might break out a deck of cards without even having the decency to pull down the window shades.

But worldly as these two breeds of Protestants undoubtedly were, they were at least consistent. The Methodists on the other hand were so unpredictable that one could never guess what kind of modernism or false doctrine they might tolerate next. And they had all kinds of members in their pews, from the great people up on Crown Hill to Baptists fallen from grace. Some Methodists were so evangelical that they even kept a mid-week prayer meeting alive, but others had so little regard for their eternal souls that they voted openly against temperance and let their children go to dances. And come election day they were so utterly untrustworthy that neither of the candidates could count on them. They were in fact so fickle in their politics they were quite capable of voting Conservative in the Dominion election and Liberal for the provincial seat.

So far as my mother was concerned there was just one good thing to be said about the Methodists. They were the best singers of the bunch, and they didn't object at all to singing old-time gospel songs that had an enthusiastic beat to them. And there was a time when the siren lure of their music almost tempted her to join the Methodist choir, though she declared she would never never have been tempted to join the church itself.

The third division of the Protestant faith was, in the firm theology of my boyhood, the Truth. And it was the whole Truth, and nothing but the Truth, and how singularly fortunate we were to be able to claim it for ourselves! Sometimes when I was still so young and so unimportant that Satan had not yet bothered to set snares of doubt for me. I would sometimes lie awake after saying my prayers at night, marvelling at how incredibly fortunate we were to be walking in the One True Light. Here we were in a world where darkness reigned on every hand, where untold millions had never even heard of the gospel, and where even in that civilized part of the earth which called itself Christian the great mass of pople was rushing hellward to destruction or everlasting punishment. And we were of that pitifully few who had been redeemed and who were gathered safe within the fold!

It didn't occur to me then that the Almighty might have been guilty of playing favourites. It had simply been predestined this way from the beginning. "Strait is the gate and narrow the way and few there be that find it," so the Bible had declared, and how easy it was for us to see the accuracy of that statement! And how fervently our parents thanked the Lord in our morning worship for calling us out of a world blind with sin to be his chosen people!

But as I grew older and Satan put a certain restlessness in me I discovered that it wasn't easy to be numbered among the chosen, especially when you were sensitive enough to resent the sting of the gang's guffaw. We were not allowed to go to the movies;

we were never allowed to dance; we must never indulge in any kind of gambling no matter how innocent the stakes; we didn't make cider or dandelion wine because these were evil and we didn't drink pop because it had the appearance of evil. We said "Oh Gee!" for "damn," and "Oh Jerusalem!" for "Goddamn." Our mother and sisters wore their hair and their skirts long, used no cosmetics, had no rings on their fingers.

The one compensation of being so strict a Fundamentalist in our village was that you didn't have to go to church — there being no church of our own kind in town. Which isn't to say that we were the only "born again" Christians in the community. There were the Latter Day Saints for instance, the Holy Rollers, some Baptists and old lady Vanderwoude whose Dutch Calvinism was so strict that she caught the rooster every Saturday night and put him under a bushel basket till Monday morning to make sure that no copulation would desecrate her Sabbath. But while all these zealous souls agreed that the fashionable churches were so lukewarm in the faith that the Almighty would surely spew them out of his mouth, it was unthinkable that these dissenters would ever consider joining forces to build a church of their own.

We children were bundled off to the Methodist Sunday School however, but not until mother had satisfied herself that the doctrine dispensed there was so general and indefinite that it couldn't possibly hurt us. But we rarely went to the church service afterwards, and the minister knew better than to try to enlist us as members. The big religious event for our family was the June camp-meeting held some seventy miles away in a tabernacle under the trees. We loaded the old Model-T with camp gear and a tent for that wonderful affair, and we were seldom disappointed with our holiday. The evangelists were generally imported from the Bible belt of the United States for the occasion. They spoke in an accent that was hard for us to follow at first, and invariably they preached in a voice which rose to a roar as the power of God came down upon them in an ever increasing torrent. The spiritual heat generated by that week in God's woods was almost enough to keep one boiling with glory for the rest of the year.

Now, when I look back at those days with a less reverent eye, it seems to me that there was at least one characteristic common to all these Protestants, and it was this: for each of them, contention was the chief source of zeal. In one terribly important matter however every Protestant worthy of the name was wholeheartedly agreed. The faith must, whatever the cost, be defended against the Catholics.

We youngsters weren't exactly clear on the theology involved; but as I recall our holy war now, it seems to me that it was based on the unshakeable conviction that, quite apart from the fact that they actually had idols in their church and were so utterly worldly that even the Anglicans seemed saints by comparison, the Catholics had a none-too-secret ambition to dominate the world. Our eternal vigilance was the price of safety. So it was that we grew up with our imaginations fired by lurid tales of how the Catholics were already storing away piles of ammunition in church basements all over the country, just waiting for that great day when the Pope would make his bid for world domination. And just to make sure that our waiting for that fateful hour didn't get too boring, on every Twelfth of July we had a great celebration on the anniversary of the Battle of the Boyne where James II, the last of England's Catholic kings, was defeated by Protestant forces led by William of Orange.

For the older people, this celebration took the form of a gala parade down Main Street with a reincarnated William astride a white horse. "King Billy," we used to call him. And he would be followed by fife and drum bands and a long parade of people dressed in white carrying orange and purple banners. Many of these marchers rarely saw the inside of any church but that didn't deter them at all from becoming beligerently devout on the Glorious Twelfth.

Some years ago in my novel *The Praying Mantis* I described a particular Orange parade which made a decided impression upon me, because that was the year our village reeve was king for the day. And since the horse which King Billie rode in all the pictures was a fiery giant who looked quite as regal as his rider, it seemed only fitting that one of the white stallions in the livery stable be given the proud assignment of leading the procession that year.

The reeve was fat, red-faced and very pompous, but he began to lose some of that pomposity when it became painfully apparent that the white stallion didn't have his mind on his business at all. It was soon discovered that the reason for the stallion's shockingly shameful behaviour was a scrawny little mare which some pagan Irish lads from up Kenilworth way had tied up to one of the hitching posts in front of the hotel. What the crowd never suspected, but what the stallion knew from the moment he got wind of her, was that the miserable little mare was in heat.

In spite of the unceremonious way our King Billie reeve sawed on the bit and insisted that he "whoa," the stallion suddenly broke into a delighted gallop as he got within range of the hotel, and nobody, not even the invincible King Billie I, could have stopped him. Once the stallion hove alongside, the mare carried out her masters' wishes to the last detail. She spread her hind legs, piddled in the dust, switched her tail furiously, backed as close to the frenzied stallion as her tie-rope would allow, winked her twitch at him, and when that still didn't induce the desired result, she piddled again.

The reeve had lost all control now, both of himself and his steed, and in a thundering voice he was calling the plunging, screaming stallion some very dramatic names.

"Are them there names in his pedigree?" an Irish-tinted voice asked from the crowd.

And it wasn't till then, I think, that we Protestants became aware of the flaming truth of the matter. This mare had been brought to town with malice aforethought. The whole thing had been carefully planned and there was no doubt as to who was guilty. Only the Irish could possess such a filthy, perverted sense of humour.

A Donnybrook would have broken out then and there if the hotel-keeper, an Irishman himself in spite of his discretion, hadn't appeared on the scene and ordered the ardent little mare towed around back to the stable.

But for a youngster, the parade and the picnic which followed were not the only events which made the Glorious Twelfth so glorious, and our celebration generally started much earlier. Tra-

ditionally, we would go into the nearest dry goods store as soon
as it opened and buy a supply of orange and purple ribbons
which would have been cut purposely for this occasion. Then we
would go up the street singing lustily:

> *Teeter, totter, grease and water*
> *Sprinkle the Dogans every one —*
> *If this won't do we'll cut 'em in two*
> *And bury them under the orange and blue!*

The vehemence with which we sang this battle song soon fired
us into true Christian soldiers and we went marching as to war
all over town looking for dogs which had committed the sin of
being owned by Catholics. These we would catch, adorn with
our ribbons and then scoot them back to their owners with a
barrage of stones and cheers.

It was a more exciting holiday than Christmas sometimes, and
often there would be fist-fights and broken heads before the day
was over. And before my time, my father can recall brawls
which were savage enough to wreck the hotel's drinking room.
Indeed, some seventy-five years ago the battle to defend the
faith cost at least one man his life.

Too bad that sort of piety is pretty well behind us now. I am
told that at the last big Orange celebration held in the old hometown the village priest turned out for the fun too, and that after
the parade and the speeches he was drafted to umpire the ball
game. Sad proof really of how dangerously low the fires of faith
are flickering today, even in a small Ontario town — proof that
in spite of the America-Back-to-God people and Billy Graham's
assembly-line restorations of the old-time religion, and all the
other movements so prayerfully determined to bring back the
faith of our fathers, the Devil is sowing more doubt than ever in
our minds. For we have to be much more certain of our belief
than we are today before we can hope to enjoy righteous hate as
much as our fathers did.

Chapter Seventeen

❖❖❖❖❖❖❖❖❖❖❖❖❖❖❖❖❖❖❖❖❖❖❖

One of my earliest memories is of my mother trying to teach me how to carry a tune. She was very patient, very persistent, but I was a difficult pupil.

"Now listen to me again," she would say. "I'll sing it the first time, then you'll sing along with me. Ready?"

Then she would sing the first line of an old gospel song called "Beulah Land":

I've reached the land of corn and wine

Only four, simple, well-defined notes, but it took days and many despairing tears to master them, and it took weeks to learn the whole first verse and the chorus. But I know now that it was a lesson I had to learn, for to mother it was almost as important to have music in the house as it was to have potatoes and meat.

Our family grew to a grand and noisy total of eight children over the years and sometimes the potatoes were frozen and there was scarcely enough meat to make soup, but I can never recall a time so bare or so desperate that we could not afford the luxury of music. The parlours of neighbouring farms often had an aura of aloof and dusty sacredness about them in those days, for it was still the tradition then to reserve that room for such occasions as funerals, or Christmases, or uncomfortably distinuished visitors. Not so with ours. Here the piano was always stacked with song sheets and hymn books, and hung on the walls above it was an ever-growing collection of instruments — three guitars, two banjos, a ukulele, a violin, a piccolo, trombone, trumpet, an alto saxophone, a concertina, a mandolin . . . .

Where we got the money for them all is a marvel to me now, for we grew up in the depression years when most of the country's cash was locked tight in the vaults of the mighty, and youth itself was a drug on the market. Often we got an instrument for little or nothing because it needed fixing and our father could fix almost anything.

We had no money for lessons either and we learned the bumbling way — from second-hand instruction books or from others who also played in the bumbling way. None of us ever became professionals. None of us ever intended to. Our music was merely wonderful enough to take our houseful of rowdy, brawling, contentious ruffians and knit us into a single voice. No wonder that for each of us, music would remain a part of our way of life long after we had begun to raise youngsters of our own. When one of my brothers lost two fingers in a buzz-saw a few years ago, his chief regret was for what this would mean to his music.

"Wouldn't mind it so much, but those were my banjo fingers," he said.

Mother had always preferred the stringed instruments because one could sing with them, and though she liked every instrument but the bagpipes, she was sure that the human voice was the loveliest music of all. There was little of social life for Mother in those days, for she was not a native to our part of the country, she belonged to no clubs, and she seemed to lack the talent for making close friends. Besides that, she discovered that the name she had married seemed to have a doubtful odour about it. When the nice ladies in town refused to let their children play with us, we thought little of the slight. Nice people's kids seldom made the best playmates anyhow. But for Mother the hurt struck deep.

She sang alto, and she had such a remarkably fine voice that it brought the village reeve up to see her one day. The reeve, who held an almost endless number of important positions in town, also happened to be the choirmaster in the Methodist Church and he was badly in need of altos. Would Mother consider coming to choir practice next Thursday?

We had no car then and she walked into town that night. Walked alone and radiant with the thought that she was no longer an outcast. But when she took the seat which the choirmaster pointed out for her in the alto section, the nice woman beside her immediately moved to the row behind.

With our ears to the stovepipe hole, we older children could hear her when she got home that night, crying on father's shoulder. She didn't go to church at all after that.

Yet Mother was devoutly religious. Indeed we, who were growing into minds of our own, found her ideas of right and wrong so strict that we had many a heated argument about them. But there was no argument about religion when we sang it together, and many a time when tempers had flared at the supper table, or when Father was quiet with worry, she would say, "How be we have a bit of a song now? The dishes can wait!"

We grew up, left home, married, did many foolish things and a few things that she was proud of. But the weekends found us all in the home parlour again, tuning up, singing. And when the time came for us to bring the first grandchildren with us, Mother did her best to teach them "Beulah Land" too.

"It's easy to learn," she would explain, "and once they have it, it's a song they'll never forget."

She had grown alarmingly forgetful herself by the time the grandchildren began to introduce the great-grandchildren. Names became increasingly hard for her to remember, but she still knew every word of the old hymns which we still sang with her every time we met.

"Just one more before you go," she would beg us. "Just one more!" And I am afraid that some of our wives and offspring were often impatient with the way we would humour her. How could they know what these old gospel songs had meant to her through all the long years of her loneliness? How could they understand that singing had been the one sure way to gather her family securely under her wing again, there to warm their faltering faith with her triumphantly greater one? How could anyone else suspect that this hymn we must sing with her before we left, was really her parting prayer for us?

This year, we said our last goodbye to Mother. She was sick and confused and a mere shadow of the beautiful woman we now remembered so guiltily. She insisted that she still knew us all, everyone, oh my yes! But when someone was cruel enough

96

to ask her to name us, she couldn't do it. She was too tired, she said.

But she wasn't too tired to sing, and the last song we sang before it was time for the car to take her to the hospital was "Beulah Land."

Oh Beulah Land! Sweet Beulah Land!
As on the highest mount I stand
And look away across the sea
Where mansions are prepared for me
And view the shining glory shore
My heav'n, my home for evermore!

It was I who suggested the song, but if Mother hadn't been able to help me with it again, I would have found it as difficult as when she had first taught it to me. But she remembered every line, every word.

Chapter Eighteen

❖❖❖❖❖❖❖❖❖❖❖❖❖❖❖❖❖❖❖❖❖❖❖❖

Of all the difficult duties which are attached to this business of parenthood, I doubt if there is any which is so perplexing as the chore of teaching our progeny just what they should say in their prayers.

There are, of course, several ready-made prayers for the very young, and for many parents these seem acceptable enough. Most popular of these (in case you have forgotten it) is the one which goes:

> Now I lay me down to sleep
> I pray the Lord my soul to keep
> Should I die before I wake
> I pray the Lord my soul to take

Now for all its gentle rhyme, I have always thought that there is a rather terrifying note in those last two lines. It has never seemed right to me to send a little girl to bed every night with the thought that Death might descend upon her in the dark of the night; that it might smother her with its fearful wings and, if her record for that day were not quite pure enough, might carry her off to some region of unspeakable horror. Neither a kindly nor sensible way, it seems to me, to acquaint a tender child with the solace of the Christian faith.

Then there are other factors which make the poem a rather unsatisfactory one to use. It lends itself too readily to certain profane parodies which hard-bitten brothers are apt to yell from the outer darkness of the hall, whilst their little sisters are down on their knees.

So for these and other reasons, the "lay me" prayer was never given much promotion at our house when our children were younger, and we were always happy when something else could be found to take its place.

I recall that one of our daughters, then a capable young miss of seven, mastered quite an extensive liturgy. From her year in French school, she learned a very musical little chant whose exact meaning I never did quite fathom, but it ended with ". . . *nom du Père, du Fils et le Saint-Esprit. Ainsi soit-il. . . ."*

Then one day, her Danish Lutheran grandmother took a silent exception to the Romanish tinge in that prayer and taught her one in good Protestant Danish to offset it. And to this pair of impressive-sounding supplications, each in another language, the less poetical wishes of the day were then added in English.

But the other little girl who shared our house then was still too young for such versatile accomplishment. Her four-year-old tongue, active as it was, had not yet shaped itself to the troublesome curves of French and Danish. Furthermore, there was an independence about her which did not let her submit too cheerfully to dogmas taught her by others. She apparently preferred to formulate her own beliefs and to find her own way of expressing them. It was not surprising therefore to note in her home-made prayers, a certain familiarity with the Almighty which was not entirely holy or dignified. There was the day, for instance, when she had been repeatedly rebuked by her mother for being untidy about the house. That night I heard her saying ". . . and God help me not to mess up this darn place."

But the part of her nightly prayer which I shall always remember longest was the place where she asked for nothing and simply gave a report on the world God had put about her. It generally went like this: "God's nice. Jesus's nice. Mommy's nice. Daddy's nice. My cat's nice. Grandma's nice. Everybody's nice. Good night everybody."

And as I listened to make sure that my own name was included in her list, I wondered what ready-made prayer could have been any better.

It would be not quite honest of me however to suggest that the less certain attitude we have toward religion in our home is likely to produce a stronger, saner faith as these children of ours grow up. I am under no such illusions, and I am a little shaken sometimes by an irreverence in them which would have been absolutely unthinkable in my father's house.

I recall for instance an evening when I had just sat down to the supper table after a particularly hard day's work and found it almost impossible to make conversation because the kids were so disgracefully noisy. I had some important matters to discuss with my wife, but every time I opened my mouth, one of the youngsters would be sure to drown me out again. Finally I could take no more. I whacked my fist on the table and at the top of my voice I yelled, "Quiet! . . . When I sit down at the head of this table, I'm God! And I want respect and silence!"

For a moment you could have heard the cat purr. Though I'm not exactly a Mr. Milquetoast in my home, an outburst as vehement as that made them catch their breath a bit. But not for long, for suddenly a bored young voice put an end to the awkward quiet by a laconic "Well, God, pass the potatoes please!"

Chapter Nineteen

❖❖❖❖❖❖❖❖❖❖❖❖❖❖❖❖❖❖❖❖❖❖❖❖

There was a popular belief in those days that only the Germans and the Dutch could make good cider, and I recall quite clearly now a certain Dutch home nearby which could always be relied upon to have a barrel of it sitting in some secluded spot in the cellar. It was a real adventure to visit that farm on a day when the old folks were away and have one of the younger Dutchmen lead you to that forbidden place. The bung always came out with a most attractive, musical energy and when you sucked the first draught it was always spiced with a deliciously strong gas which scorched your nostrils and brought the tears to your eyes.

I think that barrel always disappeared before it became truly intoxicating however, for our neighbours were never regarded as anything but the most temperate of people. Nevertheless our own people were much more than temperate. They were tee-totallers and belligerently so. Thus it was that we were never permitted any more cider than that which could be manu-factured with a kitchen food grinder, the supposition being that so small an amount would surely be consumed almost as soon as it was squeezed.

I think it was the fact that cider was given the appearance of evil at our home which made it so attractive. And there came a summer when we boys actually did get a half-gallon jug hidden away in the haymow. How many trips were made to explore the progress of that half-gallon, I cannot remember now, but at no point in the aging did the cider attain that delicious, tingling quality of the cider down at the Dutchman's place. Finally, the stuff turned completely vile and vinegary, and no matter how carefully we strained out the gray slime

102

which gathered on it, the flavour only worsened. It wasn't even a sinful flavour. It simply tasted like bad medicine.

"We've got to make a barrel of it to be any good," a brother suggested. "And we've got to put it somewhere cool."

The idea kept growing, and one day when our parents were away shopping for the season's supply of school togs we went down to one of our drinking uncles and borrowed his cider press. That uncle, I might explain, was one who used to tease Mother unmercifully about her religion, sometimes even trying to sing smutty songs for her benefit, and he was most eager to co-operate with us now.

We had an old Model-T truck that year, and we hoisted the press into that, took it home, mounted it in the barnyard behind the garage and jacked up the same Model-T to power the belt. A good many things went wrong before we discovered the right combination of mechanics, and after that we found that cutting and cleaning the apples took far more time than we could spare.

We settled finally for apples just as they came from the orchard. We didn't think there were too many worms that year anyhow. We hadn't found a suitable barrel as yet, but we cleaned out the washtub for a temporary receptacle, and for two beautiful hours that September afternoon, we made cider as it had never been made before.

But always there was the fear that we might get caught by our returning parents, and when we finally decided to cease operations for the day, we left the tub of brown juice where it was, hoisted the press into the truck, and breathed a great sigh of relief when we got it back home before there was any sign of our folks coming home.

The sigh gave way to anguish, however, as soon as we got back into our own barnyard. For there, draining the last dregs of the afternoon's labour, were two uninhibited and very grateful cows.

We must have considered those cows as a warning sign from Heaven, I think, and next year we were making cider with the kitchen grinder again.

Chapter Twenty

✤✤✤✤✤✤✤✤✤✤✤✤✤✤✤✤✤✤✤✤✤✤✤

G etting our righteous indignation in an uproar about somebody else's morals is probably the most enjoyable of our worries. So I wasn't too surprised to discover the other day that our high school staff has apparently dedicated itself to a war against immodesty among its pupils. In spite of a properly sexless school uniform prescribed for girls during the past two years, certain young ladies have a dismaying talent for finding other ways to prove themselves feminine.

There is blue eye-shadow, for instance; and their mysterious formula for gathering their lashes into rows of star points. Most horrible of all, some of them are getting their ears pierced so they may attach that peculiar kind of jewelry so dear to the ears of barbarians and young sophisticates.

That the effort is not being lost on the school's male population is now painfully evident, because an epidemic of holding hands in public has broken out.

"Can you imagine," the principal said to me, "what would have happened to you and me when we were schoolboys if we had been caught walking down the hall hanging on to some girl's hand? Even if a teacher hadn't happened along to read us the riot act, the other pupils would have hooted us right out of the school!"

But somehow, I couldn't help but recall certain adventures of my own school days that he seemed to have missed. True, I never was guilty of holding a girl's hand in the hall. I wouldn't have dreamed of such a thing. In the high school that I remember so well, the girls giggled at one end of the hall and we boys told our dirty stories at the other. And to any but the most suspicious and most practised eye, it would have appeared that one sex wasn't even aware of the other's existence.

We had our smooching parties nonetheless. There was a beautifully suitable boiler room in the basement, for instance, or if that were too crowded, one could always manage a secret meeting at noon or after four in the floury alcoves of the gristmill across the road. And speaking of immodest feminine adornment, I cannot understand why no one seems to remember the delightfully shocking day of the jazz garter, a product of the mid-twenties and one of the gaudier ornaments of the Charleston craze. Whether the garter actually kept a girl's hose up or not I can't quite remember, but certainly its chief purpose wasn't functional. It was made of many-splendoured silk and just in case the colours weren't bright enough to command attention, some of them sported bows as well.

It seems to me that girls then were divided into three clearly-defined categories. There were the utterly shameless ones who wore their jazz garters above their knees, the more timid ones who wore them below their knees, and those who, firmly renouncing the Devil and all his works, wouldn't think of wearing such a thing. The girls in this latter category generally came from the evangelically-minded homes in the village, and a jazz garter would have looked out of place on them indeed because they always wore stockings of pious black.

As might be expected, the worldly taunt of the jazz garter did not go unanswered. The various methods by which we boys tried to hijack them would hardly be of much interest to the mature kind of people who are likely to be reading this book, so let it be sufficient to say that some of us made quite a picturesque collection before the rage was over.

Others, who lived for the moment only, simply used the pilfered garters as ammunition, for the elastic in them was generally very good and if you stretched one over the end of your ruler and aimed it with a skill born of careful practice, you could snap the snout of a classmate clear across the room. There were some days indeed when this jazz garter warfare became so violent that the whole room seemed to come alive with scared butterflies the moment a teacher would turn her back.

I treated myself to a long vacation in the old home town last year, and I was rather disappointed to learn that the jazz-garter girls have turned out quite respectable after all. By that I mean that most of them raised but two or three youngsters before losing themselves in the various women's societies, the missionary circles and the Home and School Club. A few are even high up in the Conservative Party.

Come to think of it, the girls who eventually produced the biggest families were those who used to wear the black stockings.

Chapter Twenty-One

✠✠✠✠✠✠✠✠✠✠✠✠✠✠✠✠✠✠✠✠✠✠✠✠✠✠✠

Every time I drive the forty miles from this farm of mine to the city of Montreal, I pass through a total of eight subdivisions. (It may be twice that by the time this book finds a publisher.) The architecture of each of these subdivisions differs a little from all the rest and yet within each of them the houses are so completely similar that a man coming home a little too gay at night would have every excuse in the world to open the wrong door. Rows of little boxes, those streets. Boxes made of ticky-tacky, according to one of the more perceptive folk songs going the rounds now. And in the centre of all these subdivisions is a $5,000,000 regional high school where about three thousand pupils are scientifically numbered and indexed and follow courses prescribed by computer. And just in case the stereotyped background from which they come hasn't quite finished the job of making manageable conformists of them yet, each must wear a prescribed uniform of properly subdued blue and grey.

In my spare time I teach a few lessons in that school, and sometimes one of these pupils comes to me after the class, the eyes refreshingly bright for a human number, and confesses a secret weakness. "I want to be a writer someday. It's all I can think about. Is there any hope?"

I hope the Lord will forgive me for saying yes to the question but I cannot help but ask myself what chance there really is for a youngster growing up in this completely regulated, completely predictable environment – in this neighbourhood where there are no neighbours — to ever get close enough to the heart of humanity to become a writer? How, I ask myself, can he ever expect to meet the colourful kind of characters who deserve a story? The characters which were all around me when I was a lad in a rural village a half-century ago? And I find myself smiling as I recall them one by one. The hired man we once had who insisted upon milking the cows with his cotton gloves on because the feel of a naked teat in his palm was more than he could stand . . . . Old Lady Cashion who was half-blind and half-crazy and raised cabbages that never had a worm on them. Sold them too, all over town, even up on Crown Hill, until someone found out that she emptied her chamber pot on them every morning . . . . Old George Campbell who spent every evening of his life trying to perfect his perpetual-motion machine. . . . The priest with a brogue as broad as the River Shannon who owned a trotter and who insisted that the Irishman who drove it in the races would wear purple and orange. . . .

The parade seems endless.

And then there was old Gord MacDougall who for forty years or more managed to keep smiling with a wife who never gave him anything but hell. "The man who could get along with Priscilla MacDougall hasn't been born yet," so the rest of the husbands in town used to declare, but old Gord would never say anything so cruel as that. I suppose the most sarcastic remark he ever made about Priscilla was when he blamed their trouble on religion. "When something goes right," he told the boys down at the hotel one night, "She thanks God. When anything goes wrong, she blames Gord."

But if you could get him a bit more sober old Gord would tell you that their trouble was just plain incompatability. "I haven't enough income, and she hasn't enough patability!"

Old Gord's income would have been good enough however. He had as steady an income as a man could wish for in our town because he had been a section foreman on the railroad for longer than anyone could remember. Always had a roll of bills in his pocket and never had to write a cheque. Never had anything less than a two-dollar bill in that roll either. "Can't be bothered with 'ones' you see," he used to say with that low voice of his while his eyes would be looking way off with a half-smile crinkling at the corners of them. "I always give them to Prissy. Or to some other charitable institution."

It was a kind of joke with him. Almost everything was a joke to him. And one night when he was in the hotel and he began to leaf through his roll to pay for a round of drinks he suddenly whipped a one-dollar bill out of it. "Now how the hell did that get in here?" he said and trying not to smile at all he threw it on the floor and pretended not to notice when three or four tables full of men began to make a dive for it.

As for his wife's lack of "patability," old Gord was generous about that too. "If that there doctor hadn't told her that she could never have a kid she might of been all right," he said. "But once Prissy found that out — well, Prissy just isn't the kind to do things for fun, you see. She's always been the serious type, you see. . . . Yes, that's the whole trouble in a nutshell, I reckon. Tryin' to stay serious in a town like this could drive a body clean nuts, you see. . . ?"

She nagged him about almost everything. About not going to church and sneaking off down to the hotel all the time. About the sloppy way he ate and the sloppy way he dressed and the derby hat he still put on his bald head every evening to walk the dog. "Goodness gracious, Gordon, that hat must be forty years old! Why you come a courtin' me in that hat!"

"And I'm preservin' the sweet memory of it as long as I can, Prissy," he would tell her.

She nagged him because the feed he got for her hens didn't make them lay enough and the hay he bought for her Jersey was stinking with daisies; and one day out in the pasture, when that same spoiled Jersey swung her head around at the wrong time and hooked the back of old Gord's suspenders so he couldn't get himself free, Prissy came out of the back door yelling blue murder at him. "Shame and double shame. . . . What business have you got bothering my cow anyways? And what filthy language! I swear to goodness if you were small enough I'd wash your mouth out with yellow soap, I would . . . !"

They say that old Gord was just then wiping off some of the cowflap he had skidded in when Bossy shook him loose but he came up as gentle as ever. "Why I wasn't callin' your little darling any filthy names, Prissy. All I was tellin' her was that she ought to be a little more careful with those pretty little horns of hers. All I said was, "Bossy darling, if you must swing your horns around like that I'll simply have to drop my suspenders to you every time I pass."

"You're a lyin', Gordon MacDougall and you know it! Not only did you swear like a trooper at her, you kicked her too! I saw you!"

Of course the folks back home had the habit of making these stories about old Gord a little more loving than they actually were perhaps, but they say that when Prissy accused him of that he just looked at her for a little while till he got his cob pipe fired up and then he confessed. "Yes Prissy, I guess maybe I did hit her a kick or two. But you know why? No, not because she hooked my bloody suspenders but just because she gets so much more lovin' from you than I do that I was just plain jealous. . . ."

She nagged him about the stinking old pipe he smoked too and she burned every pipe she could get her hands on, "It's a filthy, filthy habit!" she said.

"Might as well smoke here as hereafter," Gord would say calmly going down the street to buy another pipe.

The nagging got worse when old Gord used to wander off sometimes and not come home until long after Priscilla was in bed. More than that old Gord suddenly developed the troublesome habit of taking off on a Saturday afternoon with his Model-T and not coming back again till Sunday night. "Just thought I'd try a little harder to give you a peaceful weekend, Prissy," he would explain. "Just struck off for a bit of trout fishing."

But he seldom brought back any trout, and when Priscilla happened to notice that on two or three occasions Rosy Kavanaugh happened to be away for the weekend too for some mysterious reason, she got terribly worked up about it. Rosy, it should be explained, was a woman of about twenty-three or twenty-four and built on rather dramatic proportions, and everybody in town knew that she could be very generous with a man. She was a good-looking, hard-working woman too, even if she did "put out," and she should have made a wonderful wife if the right man had come around at the right time. Only the wrong man had come first and left her with a baby that the welfare people took away from her, and nothing seemed to matter much to her after that.

It wasn't too hard for Priscilla to notice when Rosy didn't come home from the chicken-plucking plant, even if she wasn't in the habit of speaking to her, because Rosy's shack was only a hundred yards away on the back street and her pasture lot was back-to-back with the field where Priscilla kept her darling Bossy.

"You tell me straight, Gordon MacDougall!" she demanded. "Are you having an affair with that hussy?"

Old Gord looked up awfully surprised. "Prissy," he said gently, "you flatter me. How could a man of sixty-three — and anyhow, you know very well that no man who has a loving wife at home taking care of him proper will go tomcattin' around. . . ."

It was far from enough to pacify Priscilla, but all she could do for the rest of that summer was to watch the chimney in Rosy's shack to make sure there were no more of these weekends of coincidence. There weren't. But that didn't prevent the two women from coming very near to open warfare one August morning. Rosy, like Priscilla and many another woman who lived on the edge of town, had a cow. The grass was luxuriant and free around her, she always had a ready market for her butter and she had been raised in the tradition that a milk cow was as essential to a thrifty house as a busy woman. The only trouble with having a "house cow" in those days was that no one took fences very seriously, and neither did the cow. Hence the custom of putting the animal on the end of a long chain, one end of which was anchored into the ground with a steel stake. Sometimes, however, if the cow got tired of eating nothing but free grass she would manage to uproot her stake and wander off into trouble, dragging her chain behind her. And so it was that Priscilla went to her back door one Saturday morning in August and was horrified to see Rosy's brindle cow happily chewing her cud in the middle of the garden. The shriek Priscilla let out of her brought old Gord to the back door in his longjohns.

"Prissy!" he said, "I just don't understand you sometimes. Here you dang near shot me the other day for hittin' your Jersey a kick in the slats, and now here you're knockin' the bejasus out of that poor critter with a clothes prop . . . ! Here, let me have her chain and I'll lead her home."

But Priscilla wouldn't hear of such a thing. "Just tie her to the gate post and get the constable!" she said. "That cow doesn't move an inch further till Rosy Kavanaugh pays for that mess my garden is in! My lovely, lovely cabbages! My tomatoes! My darling petunias! What miserable kind of a cow would eat petunias anyhow . . . ? Get the constable!"

Old Gord finally persuaded her not to bother the constable about her cabbages and petunias, at least until Rosy had been given the chance to make things right.

"It'll cost her twelve dollars then! Not a cent less!" Priscilla had always been quick with figures.

And Rosy said she'd pay, though she wouldn't have the money till payday. Which didn't prove to be quite right though, because she came over with the damages that very night and looked the other cow-woman straight in the eye as she counted it out on the kitchen table. Six two-dollar bills, and Priscilla promptly put them up in the baking-powder can where she saved unexpected money for the Dorcas Mission Circle.

"But you know goddam well you're fleecing me!" Rosy said. "All the vegetables you had in that garden wouldn't be worth the half of that! What's fourteen cabbages worth anyhow?"

Old Gord eased himself in between them and told Rosy not to take it so hard because by the time she was a mellow old woman like Prissy was she'd only laugh at all this, you see.

Only Rosy didn't have to wait nearly that long to laugh because just about a week later there was Priscilla's Jersey one morning eating mixed vegetables in *her* garden. Priscilla was awfully embarrassed when old Gord broke the news to her. "Never, in all my born days did I know that cow to pull her stake before!" she said.

"It was probably that dirty old cow of Rosy's that learned her how," old Gord said. "Rosy says that she had no petunias et but there's at least two dozen cabbages gone, you see. Shall we get the constable to settle or just make her an offer?"

So the Dorcas Mission Circle didn't get the six two-dollar bills after all. It went back to Rosy who immediately parted with some of it for a crock of the best bootleg that old Gord was able to find for her. The two of them had a pretty hilarious time with that crock too that night, and even though nearly everyone else in that end of town knew about it, Priscilla was never informed.

So his wife kept on nagging him for another couple of years after that. Made him drink tea when he was dying for coffee, hid the pies and cakes on him, gave him liver when he asked her to buy steak and then boiled the liver because that was the way he hated it most. And he still kept making those smiling little comments about it all, though he did begin to stay away from the house for longer and longer times. Then when he was sixty-five the railway pensioned him off. There was a little ceremony in the station one night for him and some big shot from the C.P.R. gave him the best gold watch he had ever seen even though time wouldn't mean a damn to him from now on, and he was also given a lifetime pass. Meaning that he could go anywhere in Canada and back again now if he wanted to, and it wouldn't cost him a cent for the fare.

Shortly after that little ceremony old Gord was away for four straight days, and Priscilla, who was getting a little pale and shaky now, nearly went out of her head. "And what sort of a story have you got to tell me this time?" she asked him.

"I went and seen Winnipeg," he said. "I'd never seen the West before in my life, you see."

"A likely story! Very likely indeed!"

"I went to buy you a present, Prissy," he said. "Here's a pair of shoes I brung you!"

They were beautiful shoes and the price on the tag made her suck in her breath. Sure enough, the tag bore the name of some smart shop in Winnipeg. It should have been enough to melt her down a bit but it didn't. "You silly old galoot!" she said. "All that money and I know they're a full size too small!"

She tried them on and they were too small and old Gord put the shoes in the box and the tag in his wallet. Then he looked at the new C.P.R. watch. It was a half-hour before train time, only he didn't dare let Priscilla know what was in his mind.

So he was away another four days and this time when he handed her the shoes they were the right size. It was a good job they were, because eight days alone with no man to nag had left Priscilla so broken up that old Gord wondered if she was the same woman.

She wasn't. She was sick, and as soon as the doctor gave him the news he never left her side. She died that winter.

"Whatever she was, it wasn't her fault," old Gord said when he started going back to the hotel again. "There's no such thing as fault and never mind what the preachers say. We be what we have to be and that's all there is to it, you see?"

He didn't care who knew that he was seeing Rosy now, even though some of the proper people were calling her the town prostitute by this time, and pretty soon he was all smiles again when his drinking pals began to make jokes about the affair. Here was a woman not much more than twenty-five, and supposed to be the hottest stuff in town, and old Gord was the man who was finally taking over. It's accomplishments like that which make a man famous in a small town.

But nobody really expected them to get married and when they sneaked off in old Gord's Model-T one day the next May and came back admitting that they were married the whole village was flabbergasted. The devout people thought it an unutterable disgrace, the nice people up on Crown Hill smiled discreetly and began to remember off-colour stories for the benefit of their trusted friends, and every dirty old man in town wanted to holler a hallelujah.

But the villagers who got the most fun out of this remarkable match were the boys who knew old Gord best — his drinking buddies at the hotel. "The honest people," as my Uncle Yankee had labelled them. And when their curious and very personal questions received only the mysterious faraway eye-crinkled smile from old Gord, the conjecture which followed was almost unbearable. Especially after old Gord had left them early to be with his new wife.

"But he's sixty-six past!" they kept saying. "Almost sixty-seven. How would that go anyhow . . . ? Do you suppose it's all in his head . . . ?"

And one night after the hotel keeper shooed them out and they still hadn't come to any conclusion about the mystery, they pooled their courage and, with each admonishing the other to keep his voice down and for Godsakes not to make so much noise with his clodhoppers, they all set out to make a secret visit to old Gord's house. Which was Rosy's house too now (with her milking both of the cows).

Next Thursday when the hometown newspaper came out, there was an unusual little reply from old Gord sandwiched in between the obituaries and the advertisement for Dr. Chase's Kidney Pills.

NOTICE: *Will the people with the big feet who like to peek through my bedroom window at night please try not to step in my flower bed? Thanks. G. MacDougall.*

There were no more peeking excursions after that but the terrible curiosity still persisted and one night when they had old Gord with one drink more than usual in him, they made one last attempt to get him to talk. I think it was my Uncle Yankee who was the ringleader that time. "Come on now, Gord. We're all men and we're always honest about such things. How did it go that first night . . . ? How many times, Gord?"

Old Gord pretended at first that he had no idea in the world of what they were talking about.

So they tried another strategy. They began to ask one another the same question, making sure that old Gord heard all the more notable answers. "How many times for you George . . . ? Mike . . . ? Aloysius . . . ?"

"Five times it was for me but I was scared that night . . ." "Me? Why I was so bloody drunk I couldn't even apologize . . ." "Every hour on the hour for me. . . ." "Aw hell, boys, I went four times without even uncuntin' . . ."

And finally when the big honest talk had made a full circle, they all looked at old Gord again. "Come on now, Gord. Tell us. Tell us the truth. How many times?"

Old Gord put away the bottom of his last drink and when he stood up to go the gentle, faraway smile crinkled his eyes again. "If you must know boys, I just asked for the once. I was afraid she mightn't be used to it, you see. . . ."

Chapter Twenty-Two

❖❖❖❖❖❖❖❖❖❖❖❖❖❖❖❖❖❖❖❖❖❖❖❖❖❖❖

A few mornings ago when I was whiling away an hour or so in the Toronto Bus Depot, I was quite fascinated with the endless variety of the passengers who were waiting there with me. It seems to me that the bus companies have overlooked this aspect of the appeal of motor travel, for while we are forever being told of the infinite number of far places a bus can show us for very little money, no one has ever bothered to talk about the infinite number of unusual people you are sure to travel with.

Go by air, and your fellow passengers are pretty much the same — well-dressed, confident, unafraid to take a chance, all mysteriously important and all exhibiting that quiet kind of hurry which is the hallmark of that species of human which knows exactly where it is going and why.

Trains on the other hand are filled with solid, cautious, middle-class types who, to use their own phrase "prefer to keep one foot on the ground." Patient wives and faithful, house-broken husbands with sticky kids whooping up and down the aisle; and young couples so much in love that in no time at all they'll have sticky kids of their own; and comfortable oldsters who watch it all and smile about the days when they were in family-making business.

But when you travel by bus you never know who you will meet. Buses, on the long hauls at least, seem to be filled with the last non-conformists left in the world. With characters. Long-haired guitar pluckers, students, dirty old men, crochety old spinsters who bring their own lunch and medicines. . . . So I wasn't too surprised the other morning in the depot to see a man of seventy or so going up and down the marble steps which lead to the bus station's basement.

At first I just concluded that the men's room down there was too busy to accept any more customers, but when I saw this old boy going down and immediately coming up those steps for the fifth straight time, I became bold enough to ask him what he was trying to solve.

"Well you know," he told me in a perfectly sensible voice, "I just can't get through a day proper without first taking my quota of exercise. . . . I was a farmer before I retired, and when you've spent fifty years or more working an hour or more every morning before breakfast, well, your ham and eggs just don't seem to sit right for you unless you first work up an appetite."

My farmer friend seemed to think his appetite would be sufficiently primed now for he was rather eager to talk. I found out that he was living in an apartment, now that his wife was gone, and that whenever the boredom became intolerable, he would take the bus to one of his married sons or daughters. "I've got six of them," he said, "and four of them I can visit if I don't stay too long."

I felt a twinge of sadness when I watched the old man board the bus which would take him to some dutiful son or daughter and I couldn't help but think that in spite of all we try to do for our older folk today — in spite of the pension and our senior citizen clubs and beautifully appointed retirement homes and this new social science called geriatrics, we really have nothing yet to take the place of the days when a man could retire to the edge of town to an old house sitting on an acre or two, and raise a few pigs, keep a garden and split his own wood. And where his wife could milk a cow and make her own butter without any fear of an angry visit from the police or the Health Officer.

Chapter Twenty-Three

❖❖❖❖❖❖❖❖❖❖❖❖❖❖❖❖❖❖❖❖❖❖❖❖❖❖❖❖❖❖

Speaking of independent people and the kind of characters a story can use, I wonder whatever became of the gypsies. I am not referring to those members of that dark-skinned race who beckon at your pocket book from the flaps of fortune-telling tents at the fairs, but those mysterious individuals who frequented the side-roads of our rural countrysides some forty years ago. These were horse traders mainly although they could turn their hands to many another penny-catching skill, such as the concocting of herb medicines, the weaving of baskets, and the making of laces.

But it was the horse which was the real trademark of the gypsy of yesteryear, and a procession of these people passing through a quiet village on a summer morning was a sight which no wide-eyed youngster could ever forget.

The gypsy wagon itself was generally in the front, and this was of a type which is more easily remembered than described. Essentially, it was a small house on wheels, yet it was much more than that, for it invariably expressed the strange character of the men who had built it. Red and yellow were the most favoured colours, and often the wagon itself manifested a splendour and richness which seemed out of all proportion to the poverty of its occupants.

The gypsies of that day never stayed in one place very long. They would select some quiet sideroad on the edge of town where the grass was sufficient to provide a few days free pasturage for their string of horses, and here they would sleep beneath their caravan. Or if the family were too large, they might pitch a tent as well.

They seldom had good reputations it seems, and the sight of their bright wagon coming to a halt in the vicinity was a silent signal for the padlocking of hen-pens and tying the dog to the gatepost at night. But for all that, the gypsy camp was host to many a visitor, and many a horse changed hands before their evening campfire.

No farmer ever admitted going with the object of making a trade. He simply hitched up some doubtful horse belonging to his establishment and went over to see what was going on. To look at the horses which the gypsies had brought along was only a natural part of the evening's entertainment, and though I can never remember anyone giving a gypsy a horse that did not have some serious fault, these people nevertheless always seemed to possess at least a few horses of very fine appearance. When a visitor looked too long at one of these better nags, the results were sometimes disastrous.

The gypsy always seemed reluctant to sell such an animal. "Not that one," he would tell you making his face as honest as it could get. "I keep that one for myself. She belongs to my wagon team."

But for enough "boot" money, the gypsy was sometimes induced to change his mind, and the horse which took a visitor back home was often a far different animal than the one which had brought him. Sometimes it didn't get him home. Sometimes such a horse simply went on strike after the first mile. Sometimes he leaned back on his shafts to recover from a bout of the heaves. Sometimes he just decided to kick out the dashboard of your buggy.

If so, you took your beating quietly and waited for the next gypsy caravan. It was a game which sometimes went on for several summers.

Where these strange people came from, no one ever seemed to know. Nor have I ever heard where they spent their winters. They were a part of the summer landscape only, and when the horse began to fade from the land, they faded with it. It would be very interesting to know where they are now, and what they are trading.

Chapter Twenty-Four

❖❖❖❖❖❖❖❖❖❖❖❖❖❖❖❖❖❖❖❖❖❖❖❖❖❖❖❖

Hallowe'en isn't quite what it used to be, and few will mourn its passing. In the typical small Canadian town of twenty years ago, the night now given over to good-natured ghosts, hobgoblins and witches, was often as disastrous as a full-sized storm. Steps torn away from verandas often greeted the next morning suspended from the arms of hydro poles, gates dangled from the underside of bridges, and such sundry undesirable items as dead skunks and chicken entrails frequently found their way into the sacred precincts of churches and schools.

On one memorable occasion, I recall that a rather unpopular farmer in the community awoke to find his grain-wagon astraddle the peak of his own barn. It was a remarkable feat of engineering, and had I not been a member of the hoisting party, I should never have been able to figure out how the job could be accomplished.

I think that the churches were the first institutions which made any serious attempt to civilize this old pagan festival, and I suspect that this came from something more than the Christian duty to return good for evil. In our town at least, the church people were the nice people, and Hallowe'en was the one night of the year when all of us who had not been born so nice, could make some small attempt to even the score.

But the lavish and gay little parties held in church basements to keep the younger generation out of mischief, were only mildly successful. We partook of the good fellowship; the home-made pumpkin pie; the spook games in the cloak rooms; and then, when it was all over, we started the night in earnest.

The gentler, jollier Hallowe'en of today owes its existence to two things. The enthusiastic sponsorship of such service clubs as the Kiwanis, and the advent of modern plumbing. Youth can still yank steps and gates, and it can still stuff a dead skunk into the principal's desk, but ever since the outhouse began to disappear from the landscape, it simply hasn't been as easy to be so devilish anymore. What used to be the crowning achievement of the night is now little more than a memory. I am referring to the grand old art of outhouse-tipping which — as I mentioned in an earlier chapter — formed the traditional culmination of all proper Hallowe'en celebrations.

Needless to say the backhouses of the nice people in town — they insisted on calling a backhouse a "privy" — were the prime objects of this Satanic orgy, and many an old score was thereby satisfactorily settled. To this day I think that the greatest contribution I was ever privileged to make to the cause of education was my part in dumping the privy of one of my more memorable school teachers. "Whipper Joe," we called that teacher and just a few days before he had thrashed one of the boys in the lower room so unmercifully that the kid had to go outside afterwards to vomit.

It was miserably cold that Hallowe'en night, with a half-drizzle in the witchy air and the raspberry canes in which we were hiding seemed to have more thorns in them than the crown of Christ. We seemed to watch that backhouse for hours. Was old Joe never going to come out we wondered? He wouldn't be going to do it in the pot and throw it out the window, would he? Oh, he wouldn't be that dirty! Surely!

His wife came first and we held our breath. There wasn't even a titter when we heard noises that were comical enough to make you split. And finally old Joe himself came down the garden path, burping and farting and scratching himself.

We had planned every detail and once Joe was comfortably inside we didn't lose a second. One boy dropped the outside latch and at almost the same instant somebody even braver threw our wire noose over the top of the building, brought it down around the middle, and wired it tight. Then, just as Joe was becoming fully awakened to his horrible predicament we tipped the building over with Joe inside and uttering grammar such as we had never before heard from a teacher.

However, I remember another outhouse-tipping episode which had a very different conclusion. I think it was Tennyson who used to have a poetic trust that good would be the final goal of evil, and it occurs to me now that this particular evil escapade taught me one of the great lessons of my un-great life.

The outhouse we had selected that night belonged to one of the very "nicest" of the Ladies' Aiders. If she wasn't Madame President that year, she certainly had been sometime before, or would be soon after. It was the big job of the night and I was so intent upon helping to achieve complete success that I didn't notice the loss of my wallet until we were trying to outrun the echoes of the crash down the street. I had three dollars in that wallet, an amount I would have surrendered willingly, big as it was. But I had my identification in that wallet too.

It took a lot of courage, but next morning I humbly knocked at the door and when the good lady answered, I inquired about the wallet. She didn't scold. She didn't threaten to call the constable. She didn't even seem surprised that I should be found doing such a thing.

She merely asked, "Will you put it back up again?"

Which I did, of course, but not with the help of the same bunch who had helped me tip it. Not a single one of them would come to my rescue. I had to organize an entirely new crew. Had to pay for them too.

Chapter Twenty-Five

❖❖❖❖❖❖❖❖❖❖❖❖❖❖❖❖❖❖❖❖❖❖❖❖❖

Y esterday when I went to the bank to rescue a bum check, I was asked by the smiling young miss behind the bars if I would be interested in joining their Christmas Club. It wasn't really a Club, she explained, but a plan which the bank, with its usual tender concern for the financially inept, had devised to guarantee a Merry Christmas.

"Not this year, of course," she said. "It's a bit late for that. The idea is to pay so much a week into the Club starting now so that you'll have enough for a year from now." She shoved a glossy little pamphlet under the wicket. "How much do you think you should have for your Christmas spending anyhow? . . . $500 perhaps . . . ? . . . Well, that would cost you . . . ."

I said thanks, I'd think about it. And I have been thinking about it. I have been thinking over as many of my fifty-odd Christmases as I can recall and lingering over the happiest of them. But when I go back to those which were so softly brilliant and warm that they can still bring a tear to my eye, I have to admit that not a one of them could have cost even the first instalment of that Club the bank miss thinks I should join. And the most memorable event of all my Christmases had no connection with money at all.

Let me make this plain now. I am not saying that this event was the most exciting or the most ecstatic scene I can remember of all those tinkling, bygone Yules. Actually it seemed quite unimportant at the time. It was only later when I had begun to think for myself that I realized how clearly this very ordinary incident had shown me the intended Christmas. Not the day whose joy is generated by drink and bright packages, but the Christmas whose radiance comes from nothing more complex or costly than the act of loving one's neighbour as oneself.

But it wasn't any of the pious people who showed me that intended Christmas. It was my Uncle Bill who enjoyed so many of the interesting sins that the solid and respectable citizens of our town would scarcely speak to him.

Bill had little schooling and no particular trade. "I'm a jack-ass at all trades," he used to tell us, and I never knew him to have nearly enough money. He smoked, chewed and drank whenever he had a batch that the rats didn't get into. And his swearing was genuinely creative. "Any man who owns a Model-T *has* to swear!" he used to declare. His swearing was indeed so unique and forceful that it has made a lasting contribution to my own education.

But worst of all, Bill was openly proud of the fact that he knew how to appreciate a good woman, and sometimes when one of the more Godly females in town would sail past him on the street without so much as a hello, he would soberly turn to appraise the bobbing of her rear end with the practised eye of a livestock judge trying to make up his mind about a brood mare. And at such a time he was apt to make remarks that I didn't always comprehend.

I remember one evening when my celery-shaped teacher Miss Harbottle pranced by him like that, head in the air and tail over the dashboard, and he said to me, "Funny thing how I affect the women in this here town. But that one needn't worry none about me contaminating her. I've got more charity than most men, I reckon, but there *is* a limit you know!"

I might as well tell you now about the woman who lived with Uncle Bill. She had a husband, only no one knew exactly where he was. He had just lost himself and left his wife and a six-year-old son to shift for themselves. Our uncle was a widower then with five kids of his own. His house was one he had built himself on the tarpapered edge of town — they still call it Stumptown, up there — and it sat in the middle of a garden. Behind it were a pig house, a hen house and the inevitable Parliament Building. In the cottage itself there were only four rooms and a cellar.

"Well we're so crowded now that two more won't make no difference at all!" he told the deserted woman. "You might as well move in."

So she did, and she was there for the rest of her hardworking life. Disgraceful thing for a man and a woman to live together like that, the nice people said. And to be so utterly brazen about it too! What in the world was the world coming to anyhow?

Now then, I hear you wondering, how could a man who was so shamelessly bad, be able to know the true spirit of Christmas better than the most of us?

I think it was old lady Costigan who gave me the neatest answer to that the night she came hobbling up the road to sit at his wake. "God rest his noisy soul and protect the virgin angels!" she said when she first saw him lying there. And then when she had blown away a noseful of Irish tears she turned to me. "Say what they will of your uncle, he was the best chimney-watcher this town has ever seen!"

With Uncle Bill, other people's fires became something of an obsession. And not only did he watch chimneys, but by the time I was old enough to become aware of his dedication there was a grateful little circle of old ladies in town who had come to depend upon him for an infinite variety of household emergencies. A labourer had to work six full days a week then, but Bill's Sundays were his own. And every Sunday morning he made the rounds of his dear old friends as faithfully as if he were paid for it. He mended roofs, unplugged drains, shovelled ashes, split kindling, set rat traps — the list of chores was as long as it was unpredictable.

But I never really understood how much he meant to those forgotten souls until it was suddenly this Christmas that I wanted to tell you about. I remember it perfectly. It fell on a Sunday that year, and there were special services planned for all the churches. In our own, the Sunday School chorus was to be up in the loft with the regular choir to sing some of the anthems which Miss Harbottle had been inflicting upon us for the last month. I was in that chorus because my voice was then still like a girl's when I sang, and Miss Harbottle said it was absolutely beautiful. I thought I'd never live that down. Me, the centre man of our hockey team! Beautiful! she said, because I could sing like a girl! Me, the centre man and the *captain* of the Stumptown Stallions!

So I wasn't too sure I was going to show up in church that morning and I managed to strike out ahead of the sleigh that would take the rest of the family. There had been a blizzard the day before and I told my dad the roads were too heavy for the horses to pull the lot of us.

Uncle Bill was digging through a drift which was as high as his shovel when I got there. He was about sixty then and a little too fat for much shovelling. His face was very red. "Want a job?" he asked. "I've got a big storm in my yard."

"It's against my religion to work on the Sabbath," I said. "I'm just playing hookey from church."

Bill tossed his shovel into the woodshed. "All right," he said, "Wait till I pour some hot water into the Model-T and you can visit my old ladies with me. I can use a little help. I've got a treat for them all this morning."

It took a lot of hot water and time and swearing to wake up the Model-T but it didn't take long to get the treat ready. Five little cuts of pork from the loin of the pig he had butchered the week before and a crock-full of home-made sauerkraut. The pork was wrapped in newspaper. "We'll ration out the sauer-kraut later," Bill decided.

So that's how I met the old girls on my Uncle's Sunday morning route. "Well somebody ought to look after them, lad," he said as the Model-T went coughing and snorting through the drifts. "And I don't see nobody else bothering. Do you . . . ? I'll tell you lad, there just can't be much worse happen to you in this world than to be old and lonely and helpless all at the same time. . . ."

Mrs. Costigan didn't seem to be so desolated by her loneliness that morning though. She had already shovelled her walk, the house was full of spruce smell and there was a pot of tea steeping away on the back of her stove.

"And would you just shake the clinkers out of me furnace now?" she asked in her rich Irish brogue. "And while you're doin' that I'll cut a hunk of cake for you!"

Bill handed her the piece of pork then and asked her how much sauerkraut she wanted, and she was so happy about it all she said she would of kissed him if he'd a shaved. "Sure but there's no one can make sauerkraut like you can, Bill! It's got a flavour all its own!"

"That's because I stomp her down with my own bare feet," Bill told her. Which set her into a gale of laughter and reminded her of the story about the Irishman and the limburger cheese, but to protect my innocence she took him into the parlour to tell him that one.

Old lady McTavish wasn't at home when we called because some second cousin or other had remembered her just in time to ask her out to dinner, and I don't remember very much about Miss Kopas except that she was awfully quiet and didn't smile at any of Bill's jokes. And she didn't even thank him for the pork and kraut.

"I'm worried about her," Bill said. "I better keep a closer tab on her or she'll be parading down Main street in her nightgown again."

I remember Mrs. Finucane much better. "No Bill," she whined, "I'll have none of your sauerkraut. It always growls inside me and besides I can't abide the smell of it!" She took a piece of pork though, after she had opened all of the parcels to see which piece suited her best. "And Bill," she complained, "you couldn't have done a very good job pluggin' the leak in my roof. Sure an' I was woke up the other mornin' with it drippin' square on my comforter! It's a wonder I didn't catch peemonia out of it!"

"I'll fix your bloody roof!" Bill told her. "And here, you'll take some of my sauerkraut whether it stinks or not. It's good for what ails you!"

I supposed he might have felt rather peeved about Mrs. Finucane, but when we were heading down the road toward Mrs. Muir's he only laughed. "You take a woman like her that's had a little piddle-bunny of a husband to nag for forty years — well it must be rough on her now that he's gone. She'd go crazy if she didn't have somebody to harp at."

The road to Mrs. Muir's took us right past the church where I was supposed to be singing and we could hear the carols floating out through the vents in the stained glass windows. Bill eased the gas lever up a bit as we went by so the Model-T would make less racket. "You know I've never been in a church in my whole life," he said quietly, "less I went there to fix something. Wasn't even christened in church. Mom just waited till there was three or four of us in the arrears and then had the preacher sprinkle us out in front of the 'tata patch. Sort of curb service, you'd call it."

I didn't feel very comfortable about our calling on Mrs. Muir. We boys used to swipe pears from her tree and tease her a lot because she was forever threatening to set her dog on us. And last Hallowe'en I had been one of the brave lads who tipped her backhouse.

I was even more ashamed of myself when we got there. Bill didn't wait for her to open the door. He just knocked and hollered something and in we went. Mrs. Muir was rocking by the stove with a purple shawl around her shoulders and a piece of old fur robe over her knees. The big orange collie wagged at us from the floor at her feet. I saw now why she hadn't got up. She was so bent with rheumatism that her back was shaped like the runners of her rocker, and the joints of her brown hands made you think of the knots on a branch of oak.

Bill seemed to try unusually hard to say something funny to Mrs. Muir but she was more interested in the box full of pictures and snapshots on the little table beside her. They were mostly of the daughter who was happily married in California now, and the sons who had gone over to France in '17 and hadn't come back.

"Oh Bill!" she said with a threatening quaver, "I don't blame Emma for not coming all the way from California this year, but will you tell me why nobody seems to know that I'm here anymore? Do you know how many fowls I stuffed for their church suppers up there when I was a little younger? Or how many bazaars and quilts I helped them with? Why am I all of a sudden a nobody . . . ?"

And suddenly she began to cry and the crying wouldn't let go of her. Not even when Bill came up and put his hand on her shoulder and asked if she wouldn't let him get her a drink somewhere. It wouldn't take him long, he said.

But when he headed for the door she came out of it. "No you won't, Bill!" she said, scraping her chair around. "You know I'm temperance . . . ! Bill, before you go, I've got a present for you. It's in the top drawer of the cupboard. Will you get it, please?"

It was a pair of hand-knitted mitts, and Bill turned them over a half-dozen times before he could find anything to say. "You knitted these?" he asked. "With fingers like yours . . . ?"

He was still looking at the mitts when we were back in the Model-T again. "A pain in every stitch," he said.

The Model-T seemed to take more cranking than ever before it would respond this time, and after we had wound her up we just sat there for a while letting her get warm. And while we were waiting the church up at the corner suddenly threw open its joyful doors and people began pouring out. They were smiling, nodding heads, clapping shoulders, shaking hands. . . .

In the seat beside me, my uncle began to swear. "God damn it!" he muttered.

At first I thought that something was wrong with the car again. "Hey, for golsakes let's get out of here!" I said. "Here comes Miss Harbottle!"

But Bill's swearing only became more fervent. "God damn it to hell!" he said. "Look at them all up there, wishing Merry Christmases all over the place and not a one of them intending to do a bloody thing about it!"

Miss Harbottle was almost up to us now. "Please Uncle Bill!" I begged.

But she saw me right away and offered me another Merry Christmas. It was a very frosty one but Bill got none at all.

"Oh to hell with you too!" he roared, leaning out of the car. He called her something else too that made her mouth go into an O as if he had reached out and slapped her backside.

After school began again, Miss Harbottle had me stay in after four one night. She was very sweet to me this time, just as she had been when she told everyone what a lovely voice I had. "It wasn't that you didn't show up for the choruses that hurt me so much," she said. "But to skip church to be with that uncle of yours! Really! . . . . You know that he's not a good influence for a boy your age, don't you . . .?"

I didn't have the courage to answer her that day and I've never quite forgiven myself. So this is my answer today — my answer to you, Miss Harbottle, and to all those desperately righteous friends of yours that my uncle swore about that day. And to anybody anywhere who so cheerfully keeps wishing this lonely world a Merry Christmas without intending to do a bloody thing about it.

Which goes for you too, friend, in case it's that time of year and you've found this book in your stocking.

Chapter Twenty-Six

At the foot of main street, in a little park across from the churches, is the cenotaph. It isn't the usual bronze statue of the gloriously defiant soldier, but a wall of stone bent like a pair of arms around the plaques which try to be proud of two world wars. The stones are as different as granite can be, and the fields which gave up these stones also gave up the names they honour.

I watched the masons cracking those stones and marvelled at the splendours which the torture of the chisel brought out of them. I remember how, when they were still fresh, the names of my uncles shone so brightly that it hurt my eyes. I remember that July day in 1922 when the cenotaph was unveiled. I was ten that year, the park was crowded and my legs too short to let me see, so I found my way up through a forgotten trapdoor to the roof of Henry Irvine's General Store and, with a dozen others equally dauntless, sat with my feet dangling over the ledge of that two-storied brick building while the giddy space below tickled me with a chill which the summer heat never quite melted. I can still feel the perfect thrill of it all – the delicious fear of being so high, the excitement of the crowd beneath, the flags swelling, the soldiers snapping, the precise importance of the firing party, the bands bursting with the sun and the music that swelled in your throat.

Then the hush of the moment when old Mrs. Muir, who had been chosen to uncover the names of the glorious dead because three of her sons were among them, could only put her hands to her face and everyone was afraid at first that someone else would have to go up for her.

The grandness wasn't the same after that, even when the prayers were over and the band had begun to play again.

Nearly forty-five years have gone by since that summer when the stones and the names and the griefs were still so fresh. Now, I am back in the old hometown for a day or two, notebook at the ready, trying to understand why the relentless demon which drives a writer should keep insisting that no book about small towns can be complete without some comment about the War Memorial on Main Street.

Why should a War Memorial mean so much more to a small town than it does to a city? Is it because villagers are so old-fashioned that they are foolishly patriotic? Or are the talents and accomplishments of its sons so unimportant to the nation that fighting is the one service they are fitted for? Is there perhaps a granite something in the country character which makes the nation look to the rural village when it must find stubborn quiet and courage in order to survive?

Or is it simply that in a country village we *know* all the names? That some of these are so painfully close to us that we cannot see the aging letters of the name without seeing the lad himself, as fresh and bright-eyed as ever, and so real that one is moved to talk to him again, as if he were listening to every word.

It is Armistice Day again, lad, and the morning is full of flags and sleet and noses red with the wind. Over at the monument where your name is on one of the bronze scrolls which records a second war, there is the usual congregation, most of them shivering and not knowing quite when they should stand or when to talk and when to whisper. Near me, out here on the rim of the crowd, I see one of the mothers you must have known, trying to keep her face brave for still another year.

In front of the names, his robes flying like the banners above him, the Anglican clergyman is lifting his face as he prays for peace. I can't catch all of his words because the wind seems to have no more respect for that plea than God Himself.

There is a firing party over there too — a squad of High-landers — not quite so sharp perhaps as that first squad we watched from the top of Irvine's store. Their kilts are impatient with the standing still, their bare legs are like new iron, and their feathers make you think of cock pheasant in the spring.

They are as young and as full of the future as you were when you left us.

Only I am not thinking of the day you left so much as the day you came to us, your hair pushing your ears out, the sun peeling the freckles from your nose, your suspenders hitched with a nail behind. Your shoes didn't match and your legs were covered with marks. I thought at first they were barbed-wire marks, and then I saw the trouble in your eyes. You would never admit it, but we were pretty sure you had just come from a whipping. We knew what kind of a man your uncle was.

You asked our dad, "Need a good man to help in the hay, Henry? For a buck a week and bed and board?"

There was something so comically grown-up about you that my brothers and I began to laugh at you.

"How old are you, Jim?" Dad asked. And you said you were twelve, going on thirteen. I know now that you lied a little about that the same as you did to get into the Army. You were only eleven, a couple years younger than I was.

We three boys began to tease you then. "Aw you couldn't pull a hen off the roost or a rooster off a hen!" we said.

"I can work!" you told us.

I have often wondered since what there was about you then which made so many itch to conquer you. To my brothers and me, as well as to the big bursting houseful you had left to go to your uncle's, there was something in that unquenchable spirit of yours which seemed to them like a fire that had to be stamped into ashes.

"Have you had your breakfast yet?" Dad asked.

You said you had, and that you were all set to work. But Dad guessed that you were fibbing and took you into the kitchen. I think you ate three plates of porridge that morning and then we went out to the hayfield.

It was a sin the way we let you work that day, but you were determined to make good your boast. You were going to prove that you could work if it killed you. So we put you at the back of the wagon beneath the loader, and thought it was a joke to toss the thistles against your legs and let the hay bury you instead of clearing it away from you.

But when the last weary load went in that day and you sat down to supper still answering the banter with a smile, we knew that so far as our father was concerned you could stay with us as long as you wanted.

Your uncle came up to see us just at milking time next evening. He had a little too much beer in him as usual and he didn't bother to keep his remarks in a voice which was just for Dad. He intended this to be a public punishment.

"So you've went and got yourself a new hired man, have you Henry?" he said. "Well now, you sure must be scraping the bottom of the barrel!"

"A farmer is always scraping the bottom of the barrel," Dad said. I remember that he tried to wink at you when he sounded off like that, but you had buried your head in the flank of the cow and you were milking and you wouldn't look up.

"Well now Henry, I wouldn't want it said that I didn't warn you about this scalawag. I hate to say this about one of my own relations, but there's a hunk of the Devil in that boy! Damn near drove his parents right out of their minds, he did. Fight! Fight! Fight! Judas Priest, but I never saw nothin' like it! So I offered to have a go with him. . . . A sad day that was!"

"Don't think he can be much worse than the lads at my own table," Dad said, going right on with his milking.

"Well now Henry, if you want to keep him, more power to you. But you better let me tell you how to handle him when he gets ugly. No use tryin' to whup it out of him, Henry. Of course you can try if you want, but I could never get any surrender out of him that way. Tell you what you do though — anytime you want to make him knuckle under, just lock him in the dark somewheres!"

Your head jerked up from your pail as if you had been kicked, and when you looked at him your eyes seemed almost as big as those of your cow.

"Oh by Judas yes, Henry! He sure is scared of the dark! At our place we've got a closet upstairs for him that locks up so tight it's like a coal bin in Hell. That's what the ruckus was the other morning. Tryin' to get him into it . . . . Oh I tell you Henry, if you've just got yourself a place that's dark enough, he'll do almost anything for you. He'll crawl through a knothole and pull the hole in after him!"

You jumped up from your cow then, left your pail in the aisle and ran from the barn. You burrowed yourself into the corn-field somewhere and when Dad finally found you a couple of hours later and led you back to the house, you were still white.

"Henry," you said that night, "You let me stay here and I promise I won't fight none. No matter what anybody does. Not even if they make me mad! Cross my heart! o.k.?"

"o.k." Dad said.

Mother put you in the cot above the summer kitchen that night and Dad lighted the spare lamp, turned the wick low, and left it on the orange crate at the head of your bed.

That lamp was yours as long as you stayed with us, Jim, and sometimes we boys used to scold Dad about it. "There's never any lamp for us," we would tell him.

We got along well those next six years, Jim. Very well. And in all that time you never seemed to get over the idea that you still had to prove you could work like a man. No matter how hard the job, or how unfair it was to ask, or whether Father asked or merely hinted that it should be done, you had only one good-natured reply.

"I'll just do that, Henry! Right away!"

I wouldn't be surprised if Dad might not feel a little guilty now about the way he let you work for us, because pretty soon, the task that was too distasteful to ask any of his own sons to do, invariably fell to you. But everything was such a wonderful joke to you!

Everything but the dark.

Do you remember the time you took over the breaking of that wall-eyed colt of ours? Ah! but he was a rough one! Broke every fence in sight when you went to catch him. Broke Arthur's collar-bone when we finally got a saddle on him. And very nearly broke my knee the first time I walked within firing range of him.

Dad wanted to load him into a truck for fox meat that day. He said that he just wouldn't have anything so mean anywhere on the farm. Except for your begging, that wall-eye would have gone to the foxes too, but you said, "He's only scared, I think. How be you give me a try with him?"

I think that you couldn't have been more than fourteen that year, but within two months you were riding that colt as if he were as old as you were.

You did make mistakes, of course, and you made a big one that day you wouldn't listen to our warning and hitched that colt to the light wagon. Because in less time than it takes to tell, the wagon was kindling wood, smashed up against our new car, and the colt was on his way to the horizon, breaking fences again as he went.

When you saw the mess which had been made of our beloved Model-T and the anger playing along father's jaw you said "It's o.k. Henry if you want to whup me."

But I had just started driving that car and I was wild about what should be done to you. "Never mind the whupping!" I said. "Lock him in the root cellar. Maybe the dark will work some brains into him!"

But Dad saw the wild-bird look take hold of you and he gave me a look that was sharper than a pinch. "Just see if you can catch the colt again, lad," he said.

I can still feel a little sick about that prank the boys played on you a week or so later, and because one of my brothers was a party to the deed I have always felt that I should have tried harder to apologize for him. He wasn't alone of course. One of your own older brothers was in the gang too, along with a couple of others who were also old enough to know better.

How could they ever do such a thing? Simply because, in spite of all the poetry to the contrary, boys are essentially young barbarians, and one can never predict when they will revert to the animal instinct to search out weakness and make sport of it.

They carried you down to the culvert which takes the government ditch under the sideroad. They made very sure that neither Dad nor I knew of the plan, though I think we would have heard you had you only called for help. There were 30-inch tiles in that culvert, room enough to cram you in without any friction. You even had a little elbow-room in there, I suppose. But the devilish part of the plan was that they had brought shovels and they were going to seal both ends with earth.

And they did. They told me afterward that you didn't get hysterical; you didn't cry, and except at first, you didn't beg for mercy. But when Dad finally stumbled onto the adventure and threw the dirt away and took you by the shoulders to pull you into the light again, you shook in his hands like a sick dog. You *were* sick right after.

My brother tried to laugh it off at first. "Just thought we'd see how that trick of his old man's would work on him," he said. "We were only fooling!"

"Get up to the woodshed!" Dad said. "All three of you! I'm going to give you all the tanning of your lives!"

I don't know whether he could have done it to them or not. Maybe he wasn't man enough. But I know he certainly would have tried it if you hadn't asked him not to.

You had begun to cry a little now. "It's my fault," you said. "They would never think of things like that if I wasn't so crazy scared of the dark!"

After we had all had time to calm down and we were walking home with the cool of the night coming down soft on us, you said, "It's awful having to be scared of the dark like that, Henry! I've got to get over that someday!"

We didn't get too excited over the war news from the other side of the world those days. Europe was always full of trouble, and after all, there wasn't much that we could do about it, was there?

And then, suddenly, Canada was told that there was something she could do about it, and before we could believe it, our country was in the war too.

But it wasn't till a year later that our government decided that volunteering was not enough for the job which had to be done. Even then we thought that men would never be conscripted from the farm. An army still travelled on its stomach, didn't it?

But there came a man to the farm one day who soon set us right on that. "How many men over sixteen are working on this place?" he asked.

There were three of us that spring — you and I and father. My brothers had gone to the city to work in a munitions plant.

"For a farm this size you're allowed only one beside yourself," my father was told.

Well lad, to be honest, I could never really condemn myself for not rushing into uniform that year. I had a right to finish my schooling, didn't I? And after all I had a share in the farm.

You didn't wait long enough for anyone to have to feel awkward about it. "I'll go," you said.

The last I saw of you was when we said goodbye to you at the station the day your last leave was up — the day you looked so much like the young men over there who are now getting ready to aim their rifles at the sky. I'm sorry we had so little to say that time. Father asked if you would be sure to write us every week, and you slapped him on the shoulder. "I'll just do that, Henry!" you said.

And you did. You wrote every week for over a year. Then there came the job which had to be done by men as strong as yourself. On the other side of the Channel was a German ack-ack emplacement which was finding our planes with uncanny accuracy. There could be only one answer. Jerry must have invented a new anti-aircraft sight. Could a raiding party go over some night, cut the barrel from one of those guns and bring it back to England so Intelligence could have a look at it?

Any volunteers?

In a moment the Sergeant-Major will read off the names on the scroll over there, lad, and when he comes to yours it will take a little longer because he has to read the letters which now come after it.

The story of how you earned those letters found its way into the papers and has now been tucked away in the official histories, but your bravest deed of all is something which none of those stories will ever mention. Because to those who never knew you it must seem a mere detail that from the moment you volunteered for that raid, you knew it would have to be made on the darkest night possible.

And now there's a channel crossing not too far ahead of me and my fear of the dark is something my getting old can't seem to conquer.

When you see me coming, will you show me a light, lad?

Chapter Twenty-Seven

❧✥✤✥✤✥✤✥✤✥✤✥✤✥✤✥✤✥✤✥✤✥✤✥✤✥✤✤✥✤✥❧

All that I want this book to say really is that when it is time for me to retire, on the day when I turn this farm of mine over to younger and surer hands, I do not wish for any Riviera, no island in the sun specially subdivided for rich old men with rheumatism. Just give me a cottage on the green rim of some country village where talk is still more important than time and where there is always a good excuse for the long way round. Give me a cottage, complete with stable and strawberry patch, in some town which is still human enough to like the sound of roosters crowing in the morning and that will be enough for me.

My only regret is that I can no longer hope to find that cottage back in the village which made me what I am — the village of this book. For I have let my roots get too deep somewhere else. I have children and grandchildren who know nothing at all about the old home town, nor do they want to know. They have their own home town.

But that instinct to return to the womb is as stubborn as it is ridiculous, and long after the practical half of my brain convinced me that I could never go back, I would say to myself "All right then. When I die, I will be buried there!"

And the silly side of me built up quite a wonderful picture of how suitably magnificent such a homecoming would be. They would put a silver quill on the top of my coffin before they put me on the train, and with all the haste compatible with decorum, the old town would be told the awsome news that I was on the way home at last. The minister would have time then to put together the praise which a writer is supposed to get after he dies. And since I would have been so long away there would be few to doubt him should he find something to say, with proper restraint of course, about the great soul of me. Nor would his audience be apt to realize that had I really been a great writer, people like themselves could never have understood me.

Next day, when that fateful train would come in with me, the undertaker would certainly not be alone. The reeve would be there, and two or three of the village councillors perhaps. Maybe even a representative of the Canadian Authors' Association. Oh there would be quite an impressive gathering at the station that day . . . .

But now I see by the paper that the railway station back home was closed down last month. The local Member of Parliament did his best to convince the powers in Ottawa that this dastardly act should not be allowed to happen but it happened anyhow, and now if one of my old neighbours wants to ship something by rail he must truck it to the nearest station which the railway has condescended to leave in business. That station happens to be at Grand Valley, eleven miles down the line.

And so I must forget even this part of that dream to go back. Even when I am dead and famous I will not be coming back to that same station where on that blustery February day in the depression, with $46 in my pocket and grandma's tears on my shoulders, I promised so faithfully to make a quick success in the world and then hurry home. After all what kind of going-out would I have if that train had to dump me off at another town eleven miles away, amongst strangers and with nobody having the least concern about me except the agent waiting impatiently for someone to sign his book and thus relieve him of any further responsibility.

So, little town, I must offer my goodbye now. Also my apologies. And above all else, my thanks.